on track ...

Neil Young
1963-1970

every album, every song

Opher Goodwin

sonicbondpublishing.com

Sonicbond Publishing Limited
www.sonicbondpublishing.co.uk
Email: info@sonicbondpublishing.co.uk

First Published in the United Kingdom 2024
First Published in the United States 2024

British Library Cataloguing in Publication Data:
A Catalogue record for this book is available from the British Library

Typeset in ITC Garamond Std & ITC Avant Garde Gothic
Printed and bound in England

Graphic design and typesetting: Full Moon Media

Follow us on social media:
Twitter: https://twitter.com/SonicbondP
Instagram: www.instagram.com/sonicbondpublishing_/
Facebook: www.facebook.com/SonicbondPublishing/

Linktree QR code:

I pity the poor fool who attempts to crack the
meaning of his lyrics. It can't be done.
Jimmy McDonough

Music is not the same part of culture that it was. We would go into the spirit
world, listening, feeling and absorbing the waves of sound... (now) It's like a
cool pastime, or a toy, not like a message to the soul.
Neil Young, from his autobiography *Waging Heavy Peace*

Be great or be gone. Life is a shit sandwich; eat it or die.
David Berry

Rust never sleeps.
Neil Young

Would you like to write for Sonicbond Publishing?

At Sonicbond Publishing we are always on the look-out for authors, particularly for our two main series:

On Track. Mixing fact with in depth analysis, the On Track series examines the work of a particular musical artist or group. All genres are considered from easy listening and jazz to 60s soul to 90s pop, via rock and metal.

On Screen. This series looks at the world of film and television. Subjects considered include directors, actors and writers, as well as entire television and film series. As with the On Track series, we balance fact with analysis.

While professional writing experience would, of course, be an advantage the most important qualification is to have real enthusiasm and knowledge of your subject. First-time authors are welcomed, but the ability to write well in English is essential.

Sonicbond Publishing has distribution throughout Europe and North America, and all books are also published in E-book form. Authors will be paid a royalty based on sales of their book.

Further details are available from www.sonicbondpublishing.co.uk. To contact us, complete the contact form there or
email info@sonicbondpublishing.co.uk

on track ...

Neil Young
1963-1970

Contents

Introduction

Neil Young is the vagabond chameleon, easily bored and always searching for something new. His wild, maverick spirit and surging creative energies have always been given free rein, his commitment always total. For Neil, ever since his childhood, when he found himself moving house so many times, change has been the norm. But whatever it is he's doing, it's always 100%.

Neil is the rock 'n' roll gypsy, always on the move, never parking his caravan long in any one spot. As Neil said in his autobiography *Waging Heavy Peace:* 'I have a thing for transportation, cars, boats, trains. Travelling. I like moving'.

Fame and fortune were rarely his motivation, as he worshipped his art, the music always came first. There was never any compromise. Friendships, lovers and relationships were sacrificed on the altar of his obsessive music.

Whereas most rock musicians went into music to pull the chicks (Jimmy McDonough quotes Graham Nash in his biography *Shakey:* 'anyone who tells you that they didn't get into rock 'n' roll to get laid is lying'), that was not the case with Neil, he was the exception – Neil went into it for the music. Indeed, in the early days, there was no time for girls. Jimmy quotes Neil's mother Rassy: 'Neil didn't have any girlfriends. He was too busy playing music'.

That love of the seminal excitement of rock music never diminished. In later years, following the advent of digital sounds and the MP3, he set off on a musical crusade to take digital music back to the quality of the analogue sounds that first gave him that transcendental spiritual experience he had felt as a youth. He wants future generations to experience the delight and rapture that so moved him when he was young. He thinks they are being short-changed.

Like his lurching, rhythmic movements when straining notes out of his guitar during a performance (maybe a nod to that polio he suffered as a child?), his career has constantly lurched from one thing to another. He's burnt his way through various styles and genres with wildly different moods, as his muse latched on to a variety of obsessive interests – never predictable or safe, never with a thought for commercial impact, always giving everything, striving to connect with the muse that had infected him as a boy. If something caught his attention, he went into it full pelt. Nothing held back.

It was that constant striving that drove him to become one of the greatest songwriters and performers of the rock 'n' roll era, and certainly one of the most prolific.

He's rampaged through styles, bands and musicians like a raging comet, always looking for the next project, something he could lose himself in and become fixated on. It's a thirst that has never ceased.

Fortunately for him, his early fame and success gave him the leeway and platform to indulge. He could give free rein to his creative juices, experiment and change with little regard to pressures from labels or financial concerns, his bands, or even his fans. He had a licence to free his imagination and that's what he did. He went with that wayward wind wherever it took him.

Neil is the ultimate innovator whether in the field of folk, blues, country, grunge, rock 'n' roll, R&B, punk or electronic; he's not only tried it but made it his own in the process. That's the difference between an innovator and an imitator.

Part of his unique personality can be traced back to his roots. He's Canadian, not American, and I think that shows. He was born in Toronto in 1945, but brought up in a sleepy town in Ontario called Omemee, before relocating to Winnipeg and then back to Toronto. Following the break-up of his parents, life was unsettled. That Canadian upbringing, the loss of a father in the house, coupled with the presence of a strong, sometimes overpowering mother, helped shape him and made him what he is. The friendships, attitudes and ethos, entailed in growing up north of the border mould a different type of person and his father leaving made him more introspective, but also had the effect of giving him more freedom than he would have had if he'd stayed. His mother Rassy, though alcoholic and domineering, gave him the almost unlimited freedom and support that helped him develop.

Like many kids, myself included, Neil was ensnared by music from a very young age. Glued to the radio, whether the small transistor under his pillow or the radio in the living room that he used to dance to, he lapped up anything good he could find, from early rock 'n' roll and R&B to country and western and pop. Being in Canada put a different twist on that early exposure. Neil was knocked out by Elvis but was also enthused by all the shades of lively popular music that spilt out of the airwaves. The flat countryside that stretched right down from Canada to the Southern States meant he could receive radio stations right down a thousand miles to the Mexican border. On a good night, he could even tune in to Wolfman Jack with his wild rockin' shows. But there were also blues, country and cajun. He had access to a wide variety. Being Canadian also gave him a more British slant to what he was listening to, which included early Cliff Richard and, particularly, The Shadows with Hank Marvin's guitar playing. Neil loved the sounds Hank created with his whammy bar and echoplex. Neil's first recordings with the Squires were instrumentals in which Hank's guitar style was evident.

His father was a writer, his mother a strong personality and TV panellist and his brother Bob, a champion golfer. The whole family were strong characters. Neil's early life in Omemee was idyllic; spent out in the countryside catching pet turtles, raising chickens to sell the eggs, running wild and listening to music. That changed when his Dad left; they began moving around.

Nothing about Neil was normal. Maybe his early childhood brush with polio had subtly altered his brain. Maybe he was just more focused and driven than most. Maybe he had no safety net. From an early age, it was music or nothing. School was not where his focus was. He burned all his bridges, boats and roads.

Although he was mad about guitarists like Hank Marvin, he learnt to play on a plastic ukulele, progressing through to a proper banjo uke but not the guitar until a lot later. That polio had a big effect on him. He plays guitar right-handed but was born left-handed. Polio weakened his left-hand side, forcing him to develop his right-hand side more to compensate and become ambidextrous. That had a big impact on the way he plays and, consequently, the sounds he creates.

Riding on the overwhelming excitement of rock music, he formed a high school band called The Jades, then a whole load more – The Esquires, Stardusters, Twilighters and Classics. Right from the beginning, he sold his soul to the spirit of rock music. There were probably crossroads and contracts written in blood. School had no chance. Neil was never a scholar; his heart was elsewhere, and his school career came to an inevitable conclusion with tales (probably exaggerated) of him being thrown out for riding a motorcycle through the halls.

His first venture into the commercial world of music came with the semi-professional band he'd formed towards the end of High School called The Squires.

His mother Rassy, a tough, overbearing character, was always Neil's biggest supporter. She believed in him and provided the support and encouragement he needed. In *Waging Heavy Peace*, Neil speaks fondly: 'Rassy was the biggest supporter of my musical endeavours and believed in me from the beginning. She supplied her little car for all the Squires gigs, allowed us to practice in the living room and even lent me money to buy my instruments'.

Neil later bought a hearse that he called Mortimer Hearsebug, Mort for short. It was big enough to get the band in and transport all their equipment – the rolling tray made it easier to get heavy equipment in and out. More importantly, it helped them stand out from the other bands; not many bands drove around in a hearse – though I'm reminded of the British band Screaming Lord Sutch and the Savages. That hearse – Mort, or its successor Mort 2 – would later play a prominent part.

The Squires had a local hit with a single they put out featuring two instrumentals written by Neil – 'The Sultan' b/w 'Aurora'. It was while with The Squires that he bumped into and befriended Stephen Stills, who was playing with a band called The Company. That was a crucial component in the serendipity that led to so much more. That encounter formed the basis of a friendship and musical adventure that persists up until today. It formed the nucleus of three incredible bands: Buffalo Springfield, Crosby, Stills, Nash & Young and the Stills-Young Band. However, The Squires only lasted two years – 1963-1965 – and soon split up.

Instead of seeking to form another band, Neil decided to go solo, develop his songwriting and perform in the folk clubs. It was here that he developed his lyrical style and also met Joni Mitchell, who had a big impact on him and his writing. That encounter also led to the involvement of another character, who was destined to have a huge bearing on his music and career – his later manager, Elliot Roberts.

Neil's songwriting was beginning to take off. The Guess Who, featuring a friend from the early days, Randy Bachman (a local muso who created a unique echo effect, much coveted by Neil, by passing sound through a tape recorder and went on to form Bachman Turner Overdrive), had a Top 40 hit with one of Neil's songs, 'Flying On The Ground Is Wrong', which gave him some encouragement.

In the course of this solo period, Neil went to New York and met up with Richie Furay, who was playing folk in the clubs. Richie was smitten with Neil's 'Nowadays Clancy Can't Even Sing' and Neil taught him the song, which became a part of Richie's solo act. Richie would later share the song with Stephen Stills. This would turn out to be another vital cog in the machine that became Buffalo Springfield.

In 1966, while languishing in the clubs with poor reviews for his solo act, he was invited to join the Mynah Birds, an R&B band featuring Rick James. Shortly after Neil joined the band, they signed a deal with Motown. Things were looking up; they were recording their first album – Neil was finally making it. But Ricky, who was on the lam from the navy, was arrested and dragged off. The band fell apart, Motown dropped them and the album never got finished. Neil was at the crossroads again – more blood was required.

Neil had heard that Stills was in LA looking to form a band. The logical thing to do, obviously, was to pawn the Mynah Birds equipment, bought for them by their manager John Craig Eaton, buy a 1952 Pontiac hearse, Mort 2, and head for California where it was all happening. So that's what he and Bruce Palmer did.

Stills had been doing session work in LA and had been promised a deal if he could put a band together. He'd already recruited one member – Richie Furay. The winds of fate blew a pleasant breeze, tinged with LA smog, onto Neil's face as he sailed into Los Angeles looking for Stills. One can only imagine what was going through the minds of those young 21-year-olds: cool, hip, running on dreams and optimism. I can visualise the two of them floating down the fabled Sunset Boulevard in LA in their hearse – digging all the possibilities that lay ahead – cruising along the most famous boulevard in the world, grooving on the vibe, soaking up the scene. They were two young, hip and horny lads in the heart of where it was happening, with pockets full of possibilities, looking for fun and adventure, looking to seize every opportunity coming their way in a hearse. Pretty cool. This is where the hearse plays an important part in the story.

They searched the clubs for a week and were running out of luck and money, but there was no sign of Stills. Broke and bereft of ideas, they finally decided that the only thing left to do was to cut their losses and head back to Toronto. Neil and Bruce were downhearted, heading out of LA, dreams shattered, with one last drive down Sunset. Who should come cruising by in the opposite direction? – none other than Stephen Stills and Richie Furay. They recognised the black hearse with the Ontario plates and both realised that it could be none other than Neil. Stills threw his car into an illegal U-turn and caught up with that hearse. Neil heard this voice bellowing out, 'Neil. Is that you?' They pulled off the road into a supermarket car park. I can picture that joyous reunion. A meeting of minds. They'd finally reconnected.

Stills was super excited about putting the band together. They played Neil their arrangement of 'Nowadays Clancy Can't Even Sing' and it clicked. They dragged in Dewey Martin, already a veteran from various garage rock bands, having played with Roy Orbison and country bands like the Dillards and Patsy Cline. The line-up was complete and they set about producing music. The chemistry worked.

This was 1966, the start of acid rock and psychedelia, which seemed to gel with Dylan's folk poetry and his new electrified, thin, wild mercury sound. It was also the advent of folk/country rock (The Animals and The Byrds were creating a new musical vibe) – and that was also where the scene was at. The time was right for the Buffalo's heady mixture of folk, country, rock and psychedelia. They were in exactly the right place at the right time, with the right medicine – an accident of perfect timing.

The name of the band came about from a steamroller that was outside of the apartment they were sharing. That was it. They copied/acquired the sign from the steamroller and put it up on the wall. They were all agreed. They were Buffalo Springfield.

The band, through Stills and Palmer, had connections. Their first gig was days later at the Troubadour. Their connections then secured them an opening slot on a tour for The Dillards and The Byrds. That led to a six-week residency at the Whisky A Go Go, which led to a recording contract. After a brief bidding war between Elecktra and Warner Brothers Records, they ended up with Atlantic Records.

Finally, Neil's career had really started. That's also when a new set of problems arose. The pressures became immense: Neil started having panic attacks and full-blown seizures, which began to impact on live performances. He had fits on stage and pulled out of a number of gigs. This erratic behaviour caused friction within the band that played a big part in their future split. The tensions created by Neil's illness were exacerbated by the unequal commercial success of its two major songwriters, Neil and Stephen.

Neil wrote the first single. It bubbled under the hot hundred but was a hit in LA. Stills wrote the second single that propelled them into superstardom, a universal Top Ten hit.

That's where I came in.

It was 1967 and I was a mad music nut. I lived for rock music. I lived out there on the Thames Delta in the sleepy town of Walton-on-Thames, but my head was in London, San Francisco and Los Angeles. Cruising Walton High Street on my motorbike did not carry the same panache as cruising down Sunset Strip in an open-top Cadillac (or even a hearse).

The music was changing. Dylan had paved the way and acid and psychedelia were storming through. As a young kid in England, I was fully into the new sounds from the likes of The Yardbirds, The Who, Pretty Things, Donovan, The Beatles, The Stones and The Kinks. I was also getting into Bert Jansch and John Renbourn and was just about to discover the incredible Roy Harper. Jimi Hendrix and Cream were taking off. The West Coast scene was about to sweep in with Captain Beefheart, Country Joe and the Fish, The Mothers of Invention, Love, Jefferson Airplane, Quicksilver Messenger Service, The Doors and Big Brother & The Holding Company. The Byrds and Dylan were already going strong. The East Coast scene was also about to burst with The Fugs and The Velvet Underground. The British underground was getting into swing with Traffic, Arthur Brown, Pink Floyd, Soft Machine, Family, Fleetwood Mac, John Mayall, Chicken Shack, Tomorrow, Jethro Tull, The Deviants and Edgar Broughton, all about to grace our ears. In the mid-sixties, every night was gig night. Music was my world. There was so much going on that I didn't know who to go and see and what to buy with my limited budget of time, energy and money. These were the days when you were up all night with mates, talking, smoking and listening to albums. Sharing excitedly.

It was into this mad furore that 'For What It's Worth (Stop, Hey What's That Sound)' came bursting through. It seemed to capture the moment and reflect the chasm that had opened up between the young kids and their liberal attitudes and the older generation with their conservative values. This was the anthem for the new age – a song for the youth counterculture. That was the song that led me to the Buffalo Springfield album and subsequently on to Neil Young – his tracks on the album were the ones that really grabbed me.

That hit single was probably a huge blow to Neil's ego, though he's never said it. To have a Stills number steal the show must have been hard to swallow. The album was a success, but what followed was a period of turmoil. Palmer was deported for drug possession. Drugs and musical differences began to rear their heads. Management problems inevitably emerged (this was showbiz – everybody wanted a big slice). Personality clashes – mainly between Neil and Stephen, centred on who was leading the band and what direction to go in – began to pull them apart.

The second album saw Neil making solo contributions without the other band members. They released other singles, but couldn't emulate the success of 'For What It's Worth'. Neil's mental problems were becoming worse. He started missing gigs and left the band a number of times. A quote from *Neil Young – The Rolling Stone Files* explains what was going on in Neil's head: 'My nerves couldn't handle the trip. Everything started to go too fucking fast. It was crazy. I needed more space. There was a big problem in my head. So I quit. Then I'd come back 'cos it sounded so good. I just wasn't mature enough to deal with it'.

In 1968, to see out their contractual obligations, they produced their third and final album. It was over. Neil was once more out on his own – this time with a lot more credibility backing him up. He signed a contract with Joni

Mitchell's Reprise label, courtesy of his manager Elliot Roberts (who also managed Joni) and was up and running again.

His songwriting had developed and a solo album was recorded. Instead of opting for a simple acoustic production, they tried something more complex and used a new production technique devised to make stereo and mono more compatible – the Haeco-CSG encoding system – which had the unfortunate effect of degrading the sound. On top of that, the use of strings and other instruments cluttered the songs and buried Neil's voice, which was exactly what he wanted. After repeatedly being told by band members and management that his voice sounded strange and he should not be singing, he had a complex about the way his singing voice. Neil's lack of confidence in his vocal ability actually stemmed as far back as the early days with the Squires, when they'd only recorded the two instrumentals because they thought his voice was weird. It went on through the Buffalo Springfield, where the two managers did not like the quality of his voice and he gave over the vocal duties on a number of his own songs to Richie. Not surprisingly, this had a negative impact on Neil and that was partly to blame for the production on that first album.

That debut might not have set the world on fire, but it did set a tone. Some great names were involved in the production, with Neil himself, David Briggs, Jack Nirzsche and Ry Cooder all playing a part. It showed that the label was right behind him and that those big names had faith in his abilities (even if Ry was a trifle disparaging at the time).

Regrettably, it didn't work as well as it might have done. Perhaps they were trying too hard and something simpler would have worked better. Too many cooks, perhaps. The songs were there. The production sounded muddy and overblown, the vocals subsumed as if Neil was deliberately hiding them and everything lost its impact. I remember buying the album with big expectations, playing it quite a lot but not raving about it. It did not quite click.

I wasn't alone in not raving about that first record of Neil's. The album received mixed reviews and didn't sell as well as expected.

Undaunted, Neil picked up momentum and switched styles again. Plucking the musicians Danny Whitten, Billy Talbot and Ralph Molina out of an LA band called The Rockets, Neil set about creating a harder, rockier sound. The band seized hold of the vibe and called themselves Crazy Horse after the dynamic Native American chief. They provided Neil with a new lease on life. The band immediately went back into the studio to produce Neil's second album. The nucleus of the songs had been written in a single day, with Neil ill with a fever of 103 degrees. His brain was cooking. The music cooked, too.

The rawness of Crazy Horse seemed to give Neil the confidence to be himself. It was all about the vibe and feeling, not the precision. From that moment on, he never looked back. Neil was in full flow. There were never again any issues with his voice. Crazy Horse had freed him.

This time, the album was more favourably received and Neil's career was roaring again. I remember putting the new album on the turntable and turning the volume right up. I was smitten on the first hearing – that opening riff blew me away.

In the course of that year, things began to gather pace. Neil was in demand. His new-found confidence shone through in his solo work, too. He'd changed, others took notice and things began to happen. Neil was asked by Mike Nesmith of The Monkees, whom he had befriended in the Troubadour in 1965, to do some session work with The Monkees, which appeared on the albums *Head* and *Instant Replay*.

In 1969, Neil established himself as a solo artist and songwriter, had created a new sound with a rocking backing band and then veered back into another full-blown band situation. Out of the blue, he was asked to join Crosby, Stills & Nash, who had become one of the biggest acts on the planet. Crosby, Stills & Nash had gained enormous success with their first album *Crosby, Stills & Nash,* but had realised that they were in need of both some instrumental bite and songwriting augmentation. They looked towards Neil Young to provide that extra kick. Stephen Stills was quoted in *The Rolling Stone Files*: 'We wanted another lifeforce. I always wanted another rhythm section. Why not a guy who could do other things – write songs, play guitar, be a brother and stuff?' That move propelled Neil to a different level. Suddenly, everything was happening. He had credibility as a songwriting musician, a solo career, his own band and he was also a member of one of the biggest bands on the planet.

In many respects, the inclusion of Neil in Crosby, Stills & Nash was a strange choice for all of them. There was a strong mutual respect between Neil and Stephen, but also a strong rivalry, which had played a big part in the demise of Buffalo Springfield. They were both strong-willed characters. That was evident right from the start. When they asked Neil to play on their next album, he demanded to be given equal billing as a fully-fledged member of the group on his terms. Neil told *Rolling Stone*: 'Before I joined Crosby, Stills & Nash, I made it clear to both sides (CSN & Crazy Horse) that I belong to myself'. They buried various hatchets and agreed. The enormously successful Crosby, Stills, Nash & Young were born.

Neil was thrown into recording the follow-up album *Déjà Vu*. It heralded the start of an extremely fruitful and highly volatile career for the band, as once again, Neil and Stephen fought over musical direction and control, rekindling the incendiary relationship of the Buffalo Springfield period, with various individuals and factions splintering off and coming back together again, but which also spurred them all on to greater heights.

By this time, Neil Young and Crosby, Stills, Nash & Young had become permanent fixtures in the Opher Goodwin household. Their albums were the backdrop to many joyful, and sometimes intense, evenings with friends.

By 1970, Neil found himself in great demand. His cache was riding high. He resumed his solo career, first trying out the new songs with Crazy Horse, and then opting for a softer, more acoustic-driven approach using musicians like Stephen Stills and Nils Lofgren, to give him a more nuanced sound on his third solo album: *After The Gold Rush*. It proved to be a breakthrough album, throwing Neil into a secure position as a highly successful solo artist and giving him the freedom to virtually do as he wished.

By the end of 1970, the end of the turbulent 1960s, Neil had gone from being the member of a semi-professional covers/garage band, recording surf-styled instrumentals, through to a missed opportunity with Motown, a period in a solo wilderness, two hugely commercially successful bands and the start of a highly fruitful solo career. It seemed that whatever he turned his hand to, he came up smelling of ambrosia. Turbulent, eccentric, unique, introspective and audacious are the words that come to mind when summing up Neil in the sixties, though I could just as easily have used words like frail, sickly, insecure, anxious and introspective.

Somehow, he overcame the darker side and survived his physical and mental health crises so that, by late 1970, Neil had his fingers in many pies and was a confident, consummate performer as a solo acoustic artist, a member of an acoustic band, a member of an electric band and also fronting a highly original hard-rocking band. How many irons could any one man have in the creative inferno? Neil's life had become a balancing act.

This book sets out to give an overview of the music Neil produced during that seminal decade. I will not be dwelling on his other passions – his cars, train sets, film-making, relationships and family, except where they impinge on the music. I shall endeavour to shed light on all that music and put it in context. The incredible music-making was the foundation of a turbulent career that has wound its way through a myriad of twists and turns, fortunes and misfortunes, cul-de-sacs and highways, ups and downs, with a plethora of styles, arrangements and productions in both music and film. His was a career more varied than anyone else I know of; one brimming with creativity..

Neil has shown himself to be one of the giants to have merged from the sixties. The one consistent feature throughout this long, varied and tempestuous career has been the quality of the songwriting and music. It's been a ground-breaking burst of endless innovation and creativity that, thankfully, shows no sign of slowing down. Neil knows that rust never sleeps. It's a roller-coaster ride that I have enjoyed listening to and reading about throughout its full extent and I feel as if I've been right up there with him, revelling in the music with him.

Author's Note

As well as his solo career, Neil was a member of several ensembles during the period until 1970, most notably Buffalo Springfield and Crosby, Stills, Nash & Young. For the sake of completeness, every official track by those groups released within the timescale covered in this book has been covered regardless of how involved Neil was in those recordings.

The Squires (1963-1965)

The Squires were a Canadian R&B band influenced by the surf scene, as well as the late fifties/early sixties R&B and rock 'n' roll of the time. Neil said to *Rolling Stone*: 'The first song I ever sang in front of people was 'It Won't Be Long' (The Beatles) and then 'Money (That's What I Want)' (Barret Strong and The Beatles). That was in the Calvin High School cafeteria. My big moment'.

As a recording band, they focussed mainly on instrumentals featuring Neil's compositions influenced by The Shadows, Ventures and Fireballs; although live, they were basically a covers band playing the hits of the day, whatever the audience wanted, hustling to get gigs wherever they could. Neil explained in *Waging Heavy Peace:*

> We were doing Jimmy Reed style big time. I wrote a couple of R&B songs in that vein: 'Find Another Shoulder', 'Hello Lonely Woman' and 'Ain't It The Truth'. We were doing all these R&B-based covers: 'Hi-Heeled Sneakers', 'Walking The Dog' and 'Farmer John'.

However, because the band thought that Neil's voice was rather strange, they tended to focus on instrumentals – we, therefore, don't have recordings of Neil's early vocals. As Neil explains in *Waging Heavy Peace*: 'I had a couple of songs, one of which I called 'I Wonder'. But because I had a 'different' voice, we decided that The Squires would be an instrumental recording group'.

Over the course of their career, they played hundreds of gigs in a range of venues, anywhere that would have them: dance halls, community centres and even schools, all over the place in neighbouring towns. This is where the 1948 Buick roadmaster hearse that they nicknamed Mortimer Hearseburg – or 'Mort', for short – comes into the picture. Mort had blue carpets and black curtains with gold tassels. It died in 1965 but, after The Mynah Birds debacle, was replaced with 'Mort 2'. That hearse was destined to play a crucial role in the subsequent formation of Buffalo Springfield. Without Mort, Neil might not have had a career at all.

As Neil records in his autobiography: 'The Squires' first recording session was on 23 July 1963 at CKRC Radio in Winnipeg. I was 17 years old'. The Squires only recorded one single in 1963 for V Records. That single consisted of two instrumentals that Neil had written, but it didn't go anywhere, though it did get played on the radio. Only around 300 copies were pressed.

Ken Smyth, The Squires' drummer, was none too complimentary about the quality of the recording when talking to Jimmy McDonough, as noted in *Shakey*: 'But sonically, the record is so dim, it sounds as if it was recorded over the phone from Siberia'.

Even so, Neil was exhilarated by the experience and even more highly committed. He was looking to develop the band into a fully professional unit playing original material, but the rest of the members were not so dedicated, other things got in the way. Their families were not as supportive as Rassy.

They had begun looking towards other careers outside of music and were not as prepared to make the necessary sacrifices to break through. With all the other obligations limiting their time, they couldn't meet out-of-town commitments and the band eventually fell apart.

According to Neil, around 20 songs were demoed with Ray Dee in 1964 in the hopes of securing a record deal with London Records. But nothing came of the deal and only these few sides have surfaced.

Some of those old Squires songs were later recycled in Neil's long career. The cover of Don and Dewey's 'Farmer John', which was a standard in their repertoire, appeared in Neil's live act and was recorded for *Ragged Glory*. 'I Wonder' was adapted to become 'Don't Cry No Tears' on *Zuma* and 'Ain't It The Truth' appeared on *This Note's For You*. A number of those recordings have been gathered together on *Neil Young Archives Vol. 1 1963-72*.

'The Sultan' (Neil Young)
Personnel:
Neil Young: guitar
Allan Bates: guitar
Ken Koblun: bass
Ken Smyth: drums, gong
Produced: Bob Bradburn
Recorded at CKRC, Winnipeg, MB, 23 July 1963
Label: V Records

An unexceptional instrumental that is a product of its time, it sounds like a cross between The Ventures and The Shadows, with shades of Duane Eddy. It is pleasant and enjoyable to listen to and has a distinct surf vibe. Not bad for a 17-year-old Neil, but not something that was going to break through into a hit.

The use of the gong – intro, extro and at intervals – gives it a quirky signature that is fun. Despite its limitation, Neil was excited by it, as he related in *Shakey*: 'Then the big moment came and I heard 'The Sultan' on the radio! I was in my Mum's car with my bandmate Ken Koblun'.

'Aurora' (Neil Young)
B-side single
Personnel:
Neil Young: guitar
Allan Bates: guitar
Ken Koblun: bass
Ken Smyth: drums
Bob Bradburn: voice
Produced: Bob Bradburn
Recorded at CKRC, Winnipeg, MB, 23 July 1963
Label: V Records

Another instrumental surf-tinged pastiche of The Shadows and The Ventures with more of a spacey spaghetti western feel than the A-side. For some reason, it reminds me of the Chantays and Surfaris. The tune has a slightly faster pace with more drive but the same derivative structure. While there is no quirky gong on this, it does end with the spooky voice of the producer Bob Bradburn announcing 'Aurora'. Neil reported in *Shakey:* 'Aurora was originally called 'Imagine In Blue', but the producer wanted to put the spoken bit at the end so we changed the name'.

'I Wonder' (Neil Young) (from *Neil Young Archives Vol. 1 – 1963-72*)
Personnel:
Neil Young: guitar, vocal
Allan Bates: guitar
Ken Koblun: bass
Ken Smyth: drums
Produced: Bob Bradburn
Recorded at CKRC, Winnipeg, MB, 2 April 1964

A great precursor of 'Don't Cry No Tears' from the superb *Zuma* album. For a band that was suspicious of Neil's distinctive voice, this vocal is very much to the fore, delivered over a muffled, chugging guitar. The drums are hidden with the cymbal sound evident and there's a nice guitar solo, which is very much of its time. It's easy to see why Neil resurrected it and adapted it for *Zuma*. The melody is very strong and compulsive.

'Mustang' (Neil Young) (from *Neil Young Archives Vol. 1 1963-72*)
Personnel:
Neil Young: guitar
Allan Bates: guitar
Ken Koblun: bass
Ken Smyth: drums
Producer: Bob Bradburn
Recorded at CKRC, Winnipeg, MB, 2 April 1964

Another instrumental track very much in the style of The Shadows, with that surf edge having shades of Dick Dale. The drum and bass set up a steady driving beat. Neil picks a nice lead guitar over the top. There are some breaks to maintain interest, with some snazzy use of echo and tremolo. The track motors along fairly, as one might expect from an ode to an iconic car (or was it the horse?).

'I'll Love You Forever' (Neil Young) (from *Neil Young Archives Vol. 1 1963-72*)
Personnel:
Neil Young: guitar, vocal
Ken Koblun: bass

Bill Edmondson: drums
Producer: Ray Dee
Recorded at CJLX, Fort William, ON, 23 November 1964
A sweet juvenile love song written for Neil's first love, Pam Smith, featuring Neil's mellow distinctive vocals. It starts and ends with a loud, echoey sound of waves crashing on the shore. The band set up a shuffling beat with the occasional interjection of lead. I can't see why they had a problem with Neil's voice; the vocal has a haunting quality. The song has a pleasant melody, though the words are a bit slushy.

'(I'm A Man And) I Can't Cry' (Neil Young) (from *Neil Young Archives Vol. 1 1963-72*)
Personnel:
Neil Young: guitar, vocal
Doug Campbell: guitar
Ken Koblun: bass
Randy Peterson: drums
Producer: Neil Young
Recorded at Basement, Winnipeg, MB, 8-12 March 1965
A standard early sixties pop song with pedestrian lyrics about a teenage break-up. Intense-picked guitar begins proceedings, with the band coming in on the beat, before settling into a fast-paced drum-led song with an underlying throbbing bass. Neil's voice is controlled as the band wail 'oooh baby' after every line of the chorus and even attempt some harmonising. Once again, there is a nice guitar break.

Conclusion
All told, The Squires were exactly what they were: a young semi-professional band with some potential. Nothing more. These tracks are interesting as historical artefacts, but that's all. They are not even very original – more products of their time – but of great importance as stepping stones at the beginning of an illustrious career.

Solo Young – Unreleased

As with most of the country, Neil became heavily under the influence of Bob Dylan, but unlike many, he was just as smitten with Phil Ochs. Talking to DJ Tony Pig in 1969, Neil said, 'Phil Ochs is a genius. He's written fantastic, incredible songs. He's on the same level as Dylan in my eyes'. Neil was developing his own songwriting skills and tried his hand at going solo – it didn't go well. He worked hard around the folk circuit in Toronto and the surrounding areas for a short while but received a great deal of media criticism, which was exceedingly frustrating and sobering for the ambitious young Neil. However, he poured the angst into his songwriting, which developed a more serious, introspective quality. So, it wasn't all in vain.

One of the ventures at this time was a folk-rock band called 4 To Go – a revolutionary concept for that point in time. They rehearsed together a lot and Neil's manager tried to get them gigs, but it never happened. The world wasn't ready, at least in Toronto. There was a folk scene and a rock scene and never the twain shall meet. Just imagine. They would have preceded Buffalo Springfield with a very ahead-of-its-time sound.

In September 1965, he had an audition for Elektra Records. It featured just Neil and his acoustic guitar. A tape was made of that audition. Most of those songs from the audition were included on Neil's *Neil Young Archives Vol. 1 1963-72* release. The one remaining track – 'I Ain't Got The Blues' – was to be found on silver disc bootlegs: *Neil Young Meets Buffalo Springfield And The Squires (Unreleased Demos 1963-1966)* and *Elektra Demos 65 & More*.

Following the Bob Dylan phenomenon, the acoustic scene was burgeoning and impacting in many ways. There were a lot of developments taking place in the acoustic contemporary folk scene that were having a profound effect on musicians in all fields. Acoustic performers were being recorded and listened to more seriously. Acoustic guitar playing and songwriting were both developing at a fast pace. Neil was still more in tune with some of the developments in the British scene than most of his American contemporaries, as he states in his autobiography: 'One of the LP records I particularly loved was by Bert Jansch. His singing and guitar playing was masterful'.

Prior to the release of Neil Young's definitive *Archives Vol. 1 (1962-1972)*, the bootlegs were the only way to hear these early Neil Young tracks. Now, they've been superseded with superior quality. The only possible reason for having them would be to have that additional track, plus an outtake or two, and an unedited version of a couple of the songs.

The Comrie Smith Tapes (1965)
Personnel:
Neil Young: guitar, harmonica, vocal
Comrie Smith: guitar
Produced by: Neil Young and Comrie Smith
Recorded at 26 Golfdale, Toronto, ON, 15 October 1965

Comrie Smith was a childhood friend of Neil's. They used to walk to school together and hang out playing the music they loved – ranging from Bo Diddley, Gene Vincent and Link Wray, to The Everly Brothers, Fendermen and Roy Orbison.

In 1965, they made a tape together. A number of tracks from that tape were released on *Neil Young Archives Vol. 1 1963-72*. It seems that a few songs, 'Betty Ann', 'Don't Tell My Friends' and 'My Room Is Dark', still remain unreleased. These are the ones that were released:

'Hello Lonely Woman' (Neil Young)
This is quite a jump lyrically, stylistically and musically. We've moved away from the pop songs of The Squires into a stompin' blues with two synchronised acoustic guitars. It's only a short space of time, but Neil sounds so much older.

The two strummed guitars set up a real twelve-bar bluesy beat. Neil's voice is fuller and much more mature. He provides some great blues picking, and, towards the end, breaks into some great bluesy harmonica.

The teenage love of young romance with The Squires has been replaced by a much darker throb of sexual encounters with an older woman here. Neil sounds as if he is now familiar with her kind, too!

'Casting Me Away From You' (Neil Young)
This is again different, with the two guitars sounding jauntier (despite the subject matter) due to the higher capo placing. They are so high that they almost sound like banjos to me. Neil and Comrie capture a country feel that is reminiscent of the mood of 'Sugar Mountain', even if the pace is very different.

The lyrics record a break-up, but unlike the desperate teenage break-up in The Squires, this has a more mature feel to it. Experience has added a different dimension. She is leaving and he's upset, but not broken. This is the way life goes.

'There Goes My Babe' (Neil Young)
It sounds as if Neil is casting around for a different style. He is looking for something more relaxed, more poetic; probably the effect of the Bob Dylan influence starting to exert itself.

This starts with a slow, strummed guitar that suits the sad, wistful lyrics and sentiment. The vocal is more powerful and confident. The second guitar is plucked with ringing notes that almost sound like a doo-wop chorus, reminding me of Buddy Holly. They even harmonise on the chorus to create a very singable melody.

The Elektra Audition (1965)
Personnel:
Neil Young: guitar, vocal

Producer: Peter K. Siegal and Neil Young
Recorded at Elektra Audition Demos Records, New York City, 15 December 1965

In 1965, Neil managed to acquire an audition for Elektra Records, the prestigious home of many great artists, such as his hero Phil Ochs, Tim Buckley, Judy Collins, Fred Neil, Tom Rush and Mark Spoelstra. There was a lot riding on it. Elektra were considered a cool label. The Doors later signed to them. He says he was ushered into a tape store room, given a tape recorder and told to turn it on and let it run. It was not what he was expecting: 'In a little room by myself, with my guitar. Sitting on an amp. Couldn't even record in a real studio'. The songs were rejected.

A tape of the demos recorded for the audition shows how Neil has developed as a songwriter, singer and musician since his pop days with The Squires, although the performance is a tad forced. Not surprisingly, given the circumstances, singing to a rack of tapes in a cupboard tends not to bring out the best. It's amazing that it came out as good as it did. He's pouring everything into it.

'Sugar Mountain' (Neil Young)

This was the demo that clearly demonstrated Neil's transition into a fully-fledged singer/songwriter. The impact of Dylan and Ochs was evident in the way he used the song to tell a metaphorical story. The fabled Sugar Mountain represents the childhood he was leaving behind now that he had reached 21 and was no longer allowed in his favourite club with his friends – a song of yearning loss.

The lyrical content, sung in a whimsical fashion, concerns the pains of growing up and leaving the security of childhood behind – a lament for lost youth. Clearly, something the 21-year-old Neil was feeling at the time.

In this early version, the song is not yet fully formed: the acoustic guitar, with the capo on the 5th fret, is highly pitched, as it sets up a complex strumming pattern over which the lyrics are sung. The voice is strong and forceful, with depth and nuance. In future, the instrumentation would become more elaborate, varied and sophisticated, but this sets the tone for those later versions.

Joni Mitchell, whom Neil encountered while playing the folk circuit at this time, loved the song and wrote 'Circle Game' to complement it.

On this demo version of what is probably Neil's stand-out track from this period, the atmosphere is somewhat stark and lacking the colour of future efforts. But that works for me. I think it's a terrific version, a great performance of a great song in difficult circumstances.

'Nowadays Clancy Can't Even Sing' (Neil Young)

This is another of Neil's stand-out tracks from this period, a song that demonstrates the leaps he had made as a songwriter. The song is complex and carries a lot of emotion: 'More stream of consciousness about how it felt to be in my body at the time', said Young in his autobiography. It comes out of the difficult period that Neil found himself in, with his stalled career. The subject of the song is a strange, individualistic classmate named Ross 'Clancy' Smith, who was bullied for the outgoing way he sang hymns at school. Neil was relating his own individualism to that of his classmate by referring to the social pressures that forced people to conform and be silent.

This demo has a simple production, with just gently strummed guitar, which I find highly effective and suits the high emotion of the song.

Richie Furay loved the song the first time he heard it when Neil visited him in New York in 1965, shortly after he'd written it. He commented that, 'I thought the song was really unique'. Neil gave Richie a tape of the song. Richie learnt it and incorporated it into his own solo performances. I can see why Buffalo Springfield opted for Richie to handle the vocal on this, because of his rich, mellow tones, but I would have preferred Neil, because Neil's voice is so full of colour and emotion, and he handles the complexity of the melody, with its changes of tempo, brilliantly.

A quick look at the lyrics clearly shows the poetic quality that has now become the foundation of his songwriting. He managed to capture the pressure that bears down on any individual who dares to stand out from the crowd:

Hey, who's that stompin' all over my face?
Where's that silhouette I'm trying to trace?
Who's putting sponge in the bells I once rung?
Stealin' my gypsy before she's begun.

They might have shut Clancey up, but Neil isn't going to be stifled by the criticism. He's going to let his individuality run.

'Runaround Babe' (Neil Young)

The simple guitar strum, with Neil's vocal delivery strong and clear, works well on what is a straightforward, uncomplicated song.

The lyrical content reflects Neil's state of mind at the time. Was he going to make it as a musician or was his career faltering? 'The worry is back on me'. The lyric harks back to simpler times and reflects on the pressures that are now being heaped upon him during these hard solo days in the wilderness, struggling to get by: 'When we were young. We left our worries behind'.

The song is about the breakup with his early girlfriend Pam. He realised that they had grown apart and no longer shared the same dreams. He had to go and find his own way and so did she. Unlike The Squires, he is not devastated by this breakup. He's happy for her to go her way. It's a song about individuality and freedom: 'Don't try to be, something you're not meant to be'. He's also relating it to his own struggle for individuality.

'The Ballad Of Peggy Grover' (Neil Young)

This is yet another song with a simple strummed guitar pattern accompanying Neil's plaintiff voice. The story is a compelling tale: 'A play on words for Grover pegs, which are the best tuning pegs you can get for a guitar', said Young in his autobiography. It starts as a blues with a simple statement in a repeated line: 'Young Peggy just died today', but develops into a tale of defiance. The first verse tells of a young girl who committed suicide because of the way she looked – 'she just ran out of clothes'. It seems that 'the world just wore the peg down'. Neil says, 'Some people just can't stand no rain', the inference being that there will be cloudy days, but the sun will come out; you just have to weather the storm.

The song goes on to focus on Neil and his own pressures due to his lack of success and the criticism he was receiving: 'Don't pity me babe, I'm alright. Don't see no tears round me. I don't take no stock in the things people say'. Neil later returned to that line from the song on 'Don't Cry No Tears' from his *Zuma* album.

'The Rent Is Always Due' (Neil Young)

This is sung to an insistent acoustic guitar strum in a repeating series of riffs. The opening part is a precursor of 'I Am A Child'. It develops into some intriguing poetic lyrics concerning life. We're just passing through, we won't be remembered; life is just a performance, full of fairy-tale girls, posing guys and nondescript men in lines. You have to put on your costume and perform. There's a living to be made. None of it is real. The reality is having to pay the rent.

'Extra, Extra' (Neil Young)

Sung over a great chirpy acoustic guitar strum, Neil's voice is strong, clear and authoritative. The song tells the tale of a conversation with a down-and-out newspaper seller. Neil asks him how he got here and he replies:

When it's born it's warm.
Then it gathers strength in lies.
When it falls, it falls all over you.

He could be talking about love or life, news or conspiracy, politics or social change, or all that and more. How things can start good, go bad and then you get shat on.

'I Ain't Got The Blues' (Neil Young)

The guitar sounds a little muffled but Neil's vocal is strong and full of authority. This is a very recognisable Neil Young here. The guitar strums through interesting rhythmic patterns in this bluesy performance that is quite laid-back and subdued, but compelling. Neil gives a mature presentation; the lyrics are interesting and more sophisticated.

Conclusion

What was apparent during this period was that Neil's songwriting had taken a big leap forward: 'It happens. I don't understand it. The song feels a need for me to write it and I'm just there'. These new songs often seem ambiguous and difficult to understand. They mean different things to different people. Neil was okay with that: 'It doesn't have to make sense, just give you a feeling'.

The Mynah Birds

The Mynah Birds were a Canadian R&B band from Toronto. Over the short lifespan of the group, band members included Neil Young, Rick Matthews (better known as Ricky James), Jimmy Livingstone, Ian Goble, Rick Cameron, John Goadsby, Nick St. Nicholas, Rickman Mason, John Taylor, Bruce Palmer, Goldy McJohn, Frank Arnel, John Klassen and Neil Merryweather, a number of whom went on to find fame with West Coast bands.

In early 1966, Neil was not making ground with his solo career. The going was tough. The folk scene was proving a tough nut to crack. He was receiving much criticism and reached a dead end. His friend, the bassist Bruce Palmer, was a member of The Mynah Birds, a local Toronto R&B group featuring a young Ricky James (then called Ricky Mathews) on vocals. They'd had a minor hit with a single in 1965 – 'The Mynah Bird Hop' – the B-side of which was 'The Mynah Bird Song'. Not all that inspiring, but a reasonable R&B effort. Ricky was a hell of an R&B singer, though, known locally as 'the black Mick Jagger'. He'd ended up in Toronto, in a very white music scene, because of absconding from the navy and fleeing to Canada. That was a tale in itself. In fear of being conscripted, he had volunteered to join the navy, figuring that, as a volunteer, they'd keep him on home duties. Instead, they posted him to Vietnam, so he failed to turn up for embarkation and fled the country.

At the time, it was quite unusual to have a multiracial group. This obviously garnered attention. The band received a great deal of local interest and attracted a rich millionaire backer called John Craig Eaton, who bought them new equipment and outfits. He also managed to get them a contract with Motown Records. Neil was introduced to Ricky by Bruce Palmer, who knew that they were looking for a lead guitarist. As Jimmy McDonough records in *Shakey,* Bruce is supposed to have told Neil: 'Come and join our band. There's a negro lead singer. We do rock 'n' roll, and hey, who cares that you can only play a Gibson twelve-string and sing like a fag?'

The Mynah Birds had very pushy management – two rich kids, named Morley Shelman and John Craig Eaton, were financing instruments and costumes and were looking for a recording contract. Joining this outfit sounded much more promising than his present solo venture. Neil went for it, and shortly after, they signed a contract with Motown Records to produce an album.

Prior to the album being complete, they were going to release a single. A track was recorded, 'I've Got You In My Soul', but that was rejected due to its similarity to 'Little Girl', a track by Van Morrison's Them. Instead, they recorded a number called 'It's My Time'.

Things were looking good. Neil was at last in a professional unit with a record contract and the future looked bright. Motown, hopeful for their mainly white multiracial group, sent them to a dancing school to learn dance steps, organised outfits and had the Four Tops providing backing vocals. It was all very orchestrated and professional. They were being schooled for the big time. That's when disaster struck.

Shelman and Eaton were described as two rich kids in love with music. Nobody connected with the band, apart from Morley Shelman, knew that Ricky James had enlisted with the navy and had absconded – hence, he was a fugitive. The black Motown label were keen to break into the lucrative rock market opened up by the British invasion and saw a multiracial band as a great way forward – a powerful black singer backed by an all-white band. It could work – Tamla Motown's answer to Booker T and the MGs but with more R&B oomph. The big problem was that Motown Records were based across the border in Detroit and they wanted the band to play in the States, where Ricky was a fugitive. That might have been okay if Ricky had not had a big altercation with Shelman, who he accused, rightly, of having spent the band's Motown advance. He ended up punching the guy out. Shelman ratted to the record company and that proved to be the end of their contract and the end of the band. The album never got recorded. Ricky James found himself blacklisted and turned himself in.

Neil teamed up with Bruce Palmer. Impulsively, they sold all the rented equipment that Eaton had hired for them (As Neil says in the archives notes: 'We sold everything we had and some things we didn't have'). This was when they bought a hearse, Mort 2, loaded up with four friends and headed for Los Angeles to hunt down Stills and join his band. That was the start of something else.

Looking back, with hindsight, I find it hard to imagine a more unlikely pair than Ricky James and Neil Young. Listening to the loud, brash, soulful R&B they were producing, the togs and dance steps, I was even more amazed. That doesn't fit my image of the highly individualistic character I have come to get to know. Neil must have felt very much in need at the time, but then he did love R&B and rock 'n' roll. Perhaps it wasn't such a big step – it's just the thought of those costumes and dance routines ... Who knows? We might have been seeing Neil Young in a snazzy coloured R&B outfit, performing choreographed dance steps to R&B soul in a multiracial Motown band. That would have been something. Mind you, the band sounded hot.

'It's My Time' (Neil Young, Ricky Mathews)
1966 unreleased single
Released in 2006 on The Complete Motown Singles: Vol. 6 1966
Re-released as a single with its original B-side 'Go On And Cry' for 2012's Record Store Day
The track kicks in with a drum intro, a tambourine and a full band R&B sound, complete with lavish backing vocals courtesy of The Four Tops. It's a full-on production typical of Motown at its best, with its thumping backbeat, lavish backing vocals and bombastic brass put to very danceable R&B arrangements. Barry Gordy created an assembly line production reminiscent of the Detroit car factories; a unique, recognisable process that became a formula for churning out hits.

Ricky gives a very powerful vocal performance and the whole thing rocks.

It is obvious that the band were very much into The Rolling Stones at the time and that influence, plus the garage band history of the other members, also fed into the sound to create a really dynamic groove, especially as Neil was playing that cool-sounding Rickenbacker electric lead.

Unfortunately, the single was not released at the time and the album was not recorded. On the strength of this song, it might well have proved successful.

'Go On And Cry' (R. Dean Taylor, Rick James, Michael Valvano & John Taylor)
1966 intended B-side of 'It's My Time'
A love song which Ricky delivers in soft, mellow, velvety tones. Once again, it is very much in The Stones mode, with Neil's guitar playing high-picked notes demonstrating a bell-like quality. The track showcases a style closer to the British invasion rather than the out-and-out Motown production of 'It's My Time'. The band's backing vocals provide a fuller sound.

Two other Mynah Birds tracks were finally released on the *Motown Unreleased 1966* digital album release:

'I Got You (In My Soul)' (The Mynah Birds)
Aborted single
Wow! They really should have released this. What does it matter that it sounded too much like Them? I suppose that the sound was too raw for Tamla. This is a wailing blues number that could have been straight out of The Stones' or Them's early blues period. The drums set up a pounding beat and the bass is fierce and driving. There's a bluesy harmonica wailing all the way through and Ricky's voice is soulful and intense.

If I didn't know who this was, I'd swear it was a British blues beat group from around 1964/5. It's not a bit like a Tamla Motown number. This would have been a hit.

'I'll Wait Forever' (The Mynah Birds)
B-side of the aborted single
With its more guitar-based sound and no backing vocals, this track sounds much more like a Rolling Stones track from the mid-sixties. Neil's guitar is more to the fore and Ricky's intense, anguished vocals provide it with a driving force.

Conclusion
So that was it. Just four tracks. That's all we have of this strange fusion of talents. It was a combination that you would not have thought could have worked, but it did. The coalescing of Stones and Tamla really shouldn't be

that surprising. After The Stones' first two Chicago bluesy albums, they veered off into a very Tamla/soul period. What is striking is that Ricky James had really nailed those R&B vocals, the white backing band provided a solid garage backing, and yet were able to also create a very sophisticated Tamla sound. The four tracks are all very different. That album might have been something special. What a shame.

Buffalo Springfield

By the time Neil joined Buffalo Springfield at the tender age of 21, he was a hardened professional. He had put in the years and learned the skills. For four years, he had been learning the trade, developing his musicianship and honing his songwriting, beginning with his high school bands, like the Jades, to the pop instrumentals of the Squires through to the R&B of the Mynah Birds and a stint as a solo acoustic performer. He'd worked hard, played hundreds of gigs from school halls to folk clubs, travelled tens of thousands of miles and absorbed influence after influence. One only has to look at the chasm that there was between the early Squires' teenage love songs, like 'I'll Love You Forever' and 'I Wonder', to the poetic subtlety and nuance of 'Nowadays Clancy Can't Even Sing' and 'Flying On The Ground Is Wrong' as performed by Buffalo Springfield. It was immense.

The change seemed to come about over the course of 1965, coinciding with his solo time in the folk clubs and his exposure to and love of the songwriting of Phil Ochs and Bob Dylan. I believe it made him aware of different ways of writing songs and propelled him into experimenting, trying out different techniques, extending the possibilities and giving free rein to his imagination. In the process, he became an extraordinary songwriter. Under the influence of Dylan and The Beatles, rock music had progressed from the standard two-and-a-half-minute pop song about romance and break-up to epic sagas reflecting the full gamut of life, with its many tales and social implications. Rock music had matured and so had Neil. The newly assembled musicians who made up Buffalo Springfield brought together a variety of different styles: a hard rock double lead from the two outstanding and contrasting guitarists, Stills and Young, the folk sensibility from Neil's solo work, the country edge from Dewey and Motown funk from Bruce. The result was a new sound. In *Waging Heavy Peace*, Neil explains: 'Because of the diversity of musical roots, the band had a blend of music that was largely unknown. It was folk rock but also a kind of country blues with a rock 'n' roll edge'.

They chose their name from a steamroller parked outside their house and Buffalo Springfield was born. It all happened at pace. They had connections. Within days, they were performing, opening at the famous Troubadour. Five days later, they were on a tour opening for The Dillards and The Byrds. That is extraordinary, even accounting for the fact that they were all experienced musicians; to have gelled together, developed a working repertoire and put together an act in a matter of a few days, was no mean feat.

They impressed The Byrds so much that Chris Hillman recommended they had an audition at the fabled Whisky A Go Go. They spent the next six weeks as the house band at the Whisky. Their dynamic stage act made them instantly popular and started attracting record label interest. In his autobiography, Neil eulogises about the way he and Stephen intuitively interacted: 'Our guitar interplay was also something no one had ever heard.

Stephen and I would play these intricate parts off each other all the time that were largely improvised and people could hear that it was spontaneous'.

Things started happening really fast for Buffalo Springfield. It went to all their heads. Life became a circus and they were stars. The speed of events was hard to come to terms with: formed in early April 1966, gigging five days later, a brief tour with The Byrds and The Dillards, a seven-week stint at the Whisky, signed in June and recording in mid-July. That's pretty earth-shattering by any standards. It's hard for any level-headed adult to get their head around, let alone a 21-year-old kid. One minute, you're a nobody, and the next minute, thousands of girls are shrieking at you. Who can cope with the psychology of that?

A lot of things were going on behind the scenes: the connections that Stills had created with record producers while working as a session man in L.A. and auditioning for various bands, including the Monkees; the friendship with Mike Nesmith of the Monkees; the relationship with The Byrds (who shared some of the stylistic similarities) stemming from that short tour, the great crowd reaction and then aggressive management. It all came together.

Barry Friedman, a record producer who had been instrumental in offering Stephen Stills work if he put a band together (having known Stephen from his time with the Au Go Go Singers), took on the role of manager and brought in Dickie Davis, who had been the lighting manager with The Byrds. They funded the band with basics (food and a place to stay) and set about trying to sort out a record deal and career path for the band. It was Barry who brought in Dewey Martin. They made the mistake of consulting Charlie Greene and Barry Stone, who were experienced managers of Sonny and Cher. Charlie and Barry soon saw the potential in the band and ousted Friedman and Davis.

Following their success resulting from their seven-week stint as the house band at the famous Whiskey A Go Go, which was the in-place to go in Los Angeles, Buffalo Springfield soon built up a rabid following. With their two impressive lead guitars and great array of harmonising vocals, they were a powerful live act. This attracted the companies who were always on the lookout for talent to make money from, and with hustling from Stone and Greene, a bidding war was set up between Atlantic Records, Elektra and Warner Brothers. Soon, a deal was set up with Warner Brothers with a $12,000 advance – Buffalo Springfield were off.

It was in the summer of 1967 that they were brought to my attention. A friend of mine, Mike, was a guy I had met while doing casual work on a Friday night at a bakery. He was a long-haired student at York University, very much into the London psychedelic underground scene and West Coast acid rock. As the only two sixties freaks in the place, it was natural that we gravitated together. It was Mike who introduced me to the wonders of Captain Beefheart, Country Joe And The Fish, Quicksilver Messenger Service, The Doors and Love. We'd spend hours sitting in his room playing albums and discussing the music, the scene, the attitudes and the news.

Mike seemed to have special antennae. The underground scene was only just starting up and was not greatly publicised – no internet back then. The only real radio show that ever focussed on it was John Peel, with his wonderful Perfumed Garden. But Mike had his ear to the ground, and, time and time again, came up with all these fabulous debut albums by exotic West Coast bands. It seemed that every week, he'd appear with some new band with an incredibly different sound.

At the beginning of 1967, he played Buffalo Springfield to me, and I was hooked. When the fabulous 'For What It's Worth (Stop, Hey What's That Sound)' single came out, I was even more enamoured. But as the band, unlike all the other West Coast units, failed to tour Britain, I never got to see them perform live during the brief period of their existence.

No sooner were they off than they came crashing down. Right from the start, there was friction between Stills and Young – the cowboy and the Indian. While they both respected each other massively, they vied for leadership and argued over the direction the band should go in and what material they should record. Stills said that Neil wanted to perform folk songs in a rock band. It's probably pretty accurate.

On top of that, there was a lot of friction with management, unhappiness with the recording quality of their material, harassment and altercations with the police, arrests and even imprisonment, along with other internal strife within the band. The final straw was Palmer being deported for marijuana possession. In *Waging Heavy Peace,* Neil laments the loss of Bruce: 'That was why we broke up. All that fighting was because we lost Bruce. If he had stayed in, we'd probably still be together today. But losing Bruce broke our hearts. It's all about chemistry. Love and chemistry'.

Neil began to pull apart from the band and not carry out live duties, his place being taken by David Crosby and Doug Hastings. Sometimes, Stephen would have to cover the lead guitar parts by himself. By the time of the second album, the band members were recording their tracks without the others. Neil finally left the band in the summer of 1967.

In hindsight, it's a wonder that Neil Young ever fitted in with Buffalo Springfield. His songs were very different, edgy and experimental. Stills and Furay were more orthodox. Neil did not produce songs that the other members of the band could easily harmonise with. They liked to create flowing, beautiful country-flavoured songs in a more commercial, standard format. Neil gave them a rougher edge, trying out things and extending the possibilities. That's why they really needed him. He gave them substance.

Buffalo Springfield (1966)

Personnel:
Neil Young: vocals, guitars, harmonica, piano
Stephen Stills: vocals, guitars, harmonica, piano
Richie Furay: vocals, rhythm guitar
Bruce Palmer: bass guitar
Dewey Martin: drums, backing vocals
Produced by Charles Greene, Brian Stone
Engineered by Tom May, Doc Siegel, James Hilton, Stan Ross
Sandy Dvore: design
Henry Diltz, Ivan Nagy: photography
Recorded at Columbia Studios Hollywood and Goldstar Studio, L.A.
Record label: Atco Records
Chart positions: US: 80, UK: 43

The recording sessions to produce the first album and single began in mid-July. Stephen Stills and Neil were solely responsible for the songwriting. There was talk of this being the first Supergroup, but that can only be applied in hindsight. At the time, despite their obvious talents, none of the members of the band had been very successful. Buffalo Springfield would propel them into stardom.

The recording took place at the Gold Star Studios, which had previously been used by both Phil Spector and The Beach Boys. Unfortunately, the band allowed their managers, Brian Stone and Charles Greene, to produce the album. Neither of them had any experience of production and the end result fell short of what the band were after. They felt it did not adequately capture the strength of their live act. The band wanted to re-record, but the record company, with one eye on the Christmas market, wanted the 'product' out and refused.

The band must have, like previous bands, had some reservations concerning Neil's distinctive voice because he only took the lead vocal on two of the five songs he had on the album. Richie Furay did the honours. Richie had been a great admirer of Neil's songs and had incorporated at least one of them into his solo act prior to the Buffalo's forming, so that seemed appropriate on one level, but I bet it rankled with Neil. The criticism of Neil's distinctive voice cut deep. It had started with The Squires and persisted through Buffalo Springfield, and even extended into his first solo album when, suffering from a complex about the way his voice sounded, he had tried to bury it in the mix. Richie's voice is very mellow and he brings out the beauty of the melody in Neil's songs, but I think Neil's vocals would have made them more distinctive and emotive. Swings and roundabouts.

The front cover, designed by Sandy Dvore and using photos from photographer Henry Diltz, features a big heading in white on a slab of black announcing BUFFALO SPRINGFIELD with what looks like strips of coloured contact prints of the band members in three vertical rows. Very modern (for the time) and distinctive, (a tad reminiscent of the cover of The Beatles' *A Hard Day's Night*).

'Go And Say Goodbye' (Stephen Stills)

Stephen Stills sets the pace on this jaunty, country-tinged intro to the album. The track sounds extremely Byrds-like. Following Stills' guitar intro, Neil comes in with some precise, nicely picked lead and effective double-stopping (a guitar technique in which two strings are plucked simultaneously), which gives the track some edge.

Stephen and Richie deftly handle the vocals, nicely harmonising. The upbeat feel of the music is a little at odds with the sentiments of the lyrics. This takes the form of advice from a friend to bite the bullet and end the relationship, not to be a coward and hang on when it's over for fear of making her cry. The message is blunt. It makes for a bright start to the album, even though they have just started and are already saying farewell!

The track formed the B-side of the first single.

'Sit Down I Think I Love You' (Stephen Stills)

A change of tone for the second outing – a slower pace with a catchy melody. A Stephen Stills love song in a very typical mid-sixties folk-rock style. Once again, Stephen and Richie's voices blend together well. The pause in the vocal is very effective.

There is some exceptional guitar interplay. The middle eight comes in with some fuzzed-up guitar followed by Neil's high-pitched jingly guitar notes. The interaction is superb.

The title says it all. We've gone from a goodbye to a hello.

'Leave' (Stephen Stills)

The drums kick in, followed closely by Neil's monster guitar and we're into a much heavier electric rock track. There's nothing folk-rock about this. The drums pound, the bass throbs and Neil's guitar kicks ass and tears it up with shrill guitar notes. You wouldn't believe that it's the same band as on the track before – this is powerful. The message is as harsh as the music: the relationship is over – just leave. The track ends on a savage, prolonged vocal note.

'Nowadays Clancy Can't Even Sing' (Neil Young)

Following three quite varied Stephen Stills numbers, we hit our first Neil Young composition and probably the stand-out track on the album. There are not too many people who can create a song as beautiful and poignant as this out of an incident of bullying and social pressure. But this band can. Buffalo Springfield took the song about Neil's school friend, Ross 'Clancey' Smith, who was bullied because of the way he sang hymns and pressured so much that he couldn't sing anymore, and transformed it into something delicate, haunting and sensual. The song is a reflection of the social pressures Neil fell under when he was at school. Many of his fellow students were exceedingly conservative and intolerant of anybody 'different', such as Neil and Ross, and the school and society had a clear route for how life should proceed. Neil felt himself to be a maverick outsider. He didn't fit the mould and rebelled against it.

Neil's demo of the song, as it appeared on the Comrie Smith tape, is excellent and raw. This version has been polished into a gem. Richie's delicate singing, with Stephen coming in to join him on harmonies, coupled with the changes in tempo and time signatures, creates an emotional masterpiece that tugs at the heartstrings. Bruce Palmer's underlying bass patterns complement perfectly. It builds and ebbs into an effortless flow – sheer magic. I am left with one loose thought: would it have sounded as good, or even better, if Neil had sung the vocals here? Was this a group decision, demonstrating a concern about the sound of Neil's voice or Neil's own insecurity? Or was it the management/producers' decision?

Perhaps it just came about through circumstance. Richie had loved the song the first time Neil had played it to him in New York and he'd incorporated it into his solo act. He was used to singing it.

This was chosen as the first single off the album and made a bit of a splash in L.A. but failed to break into the Top 100. There's no justice. Neil thought that it was actually too quirky and different to be a single.

'Hot Dusty Roads' (Stephen Stills)

We're back with another Stills composition, another rocky number with a rolling pace. Stephen's vocal is authoritative and precise as the song rambles along nicely, with some fine stinging guitar notes thrown in.

He's telling us that he's a city boy. He's got no time for the hot, dusty roads of the countryside. He wants to be comfortable indoors, sitting down in a comfy chair with friends, talking about life and what it's all about. So come on, girl, knock on the door, take off your shoes, make yourself comfortable – you'll find him there.

'Everybody's Wrong' (Stephen Stills)

This is an interesting song about fake news before there was even any mention of fake news. Who knows what to believe? Are we being deceived? There are too many words going down, echoing off the walls. You set out to live your life and find out you've been bought. Was he thinking about the music business? All is not what it seems.

This is another fast-paced rockin' tune in the Mike Nesmith style. Stephen had tried out for The Monkees and Mike had been a friend since Stephen moved to L.A. The influence is clear. The track starts with drums and tambourine as the band set a good pace before ending with a thrash of chords and an oscillating echo.

'Flying On The Ground Is Wrong' (Neil Young)

In my opinion, the album seems to comprise two halves. Side one is the Stephen Stills side and side two is the Neil Young showcase. For me, Neil's songs tend to be more introspective and interesting, whereas Stephen's songs are more commercial and straightforward. But that's just my impression.

Another song written by Neil where Richie takes the lead vocal, this slow, tender, whimsical song is about a break-up with a girl he can really relate to. She's from his part of town, but he's changing, getting into the alternate scene and drugs, and she's remaining straight. As Neil said in an interview with *Rolling Stone*: 'It's a drug song. It's about being straight and taking drugs. We can't be together because we're too different. I love you, but you're not with me'. The time wasn't quite right – she was leaving.

The band provide a solid foundation, the bass weaves and Neil's high-pitched guitar lays a complex bed of picked notes. Ritchie's voice is soft and mellow, capturing the poignancy of the poetic lyrics, but I still would have preferred to hear Neil's expressive voice interpreting his own song.

I remember some controversy in the media at the time regarding the lyrics; 'flying on the ground is wrong' was made out to be an antidrug inference. They didn't quite get it, did they? At the time, a number of bands were playing to their underground, drug-using audience and putting drug references into their lyrics. The conservative media banned songs with overt references but were not hip to the more colloquial slang and subtle references. The controversy was concerning whether the song lyric was anti-drug. In actual fact, it wasn't. It highlighted the rift that had grown between himself and Pam, his early girlfriend, regarding Neil's increasing drug use and way of life. Pam wasn't into that. So, they split up. In the lyric, Neil is explaining that he had changed and developed into something else, and smoking dope was part of that; if she couldn't make that leap, then sadly, their relationship was over. Overall, this is another of Neil's poetic masterpieces, showcasing subtle lyrics and emotional intensity.

'Burned' (Neil Young)

An upbeat Neil Young number, a huge sound is created by the thumping, funky bass high in the mix and Neil letting loose with a cascade of high notes. This time, Neil is trusted with the vocals, with harmony support from Stephen and Richie. With its infectious, catchy chorus, this was released as the second single off the album and could easily have been a Top Ten hit if it had received the right airplay. It's full of energy and features an unusual jangly barroom piano middle eight that sounds more like a harpsichord to me.

Interestingly, the theme of the song is somewhat at odds with the arrangement. In his autobiography, Neil says that wrote it about 'having a seizure'.

'Do I Have To Come Right Out And Say It' (Neil Young)

Quite an unusual Neil Young offering for this period, this a straightforward love song, mellow and melodic, nothing quirky or complex about it, just beautiful. Richie does it full justice with his rich, emotive vocal, amply assisted by some sublime harmonising. There is some great folk-rock guitar (folk chords combined with the energy and rhythm of rock) in there, with a wonderful cameo guitar solo.

This was the B-side to 'For What It's Worth'. Some have said that it should have been a double A-side.

'Baby Don't Scold Me' (Stephen Stills)

Stephen creates a guitar-driven British beat sound on this track, complete with a guitar homage to The Beatles' 'Daytripper'. His assured voice is amply supported by Richie's harmonies. The track was written following an argument with his then-girlfriend Donna Port.

After the song 'For What It's Worth' hit the charts, the album was re-pressed. 'For What It's Worth' was given star billing as the first track and this one was sacrificed. I'm not sure why they would do that. It's a perfectly good track and the album could easily have accommodated an extra. They could have just added the single.

'Out Of My Mind' (Neil Young)

The producers finally let Neil loose for his second vocal outing on the album and a brilliant job he does, too. The song is so slow it's almost a dirge, but no worse for that. It starts with a quirky, distorted guitar – Neil with his new Leslie effect. A thumping drum and bass punctuate the song, which comes over as very grungish with a melancholy quality. The result is an acid-drenched piece of folk rock. Neil's distinctive voice is backed up with some outstanding harmony work from Richie and Stephen.

The lyrics are extremely moving with this drug-laden play on words. Is Neil already fed up with the fame, with the artificial world of pop star life, with limousines and screaming fans, or is he peering into the near future? Whatever. The unreality is sending him out of his mind. The play on different interpretations of being out of his mind is the basis of the song. There is the creativity of the song being conceived out of his mind alongside the allusion of being stoned out of his mind.

One of the outstanding tracks on the album for me. A psychedelic masterpiece.

'Pay The Price' (Stephen Stills)

A commercial pop song from Stephen based on a repeating guitar riff, steady drums and a throbbing bass pattern from Bruce Palmer. The second guitar from Neil overlays with higher-pitched plucked notes.

The song is about the perennial problem of a third person entering the relationship. He's telling her she's got to choose and accept the consequences. She's got to pay the price for the hurt she's causing. The song stands on the impact of that repeating last line, 'pay the price'.

Singles
'Nowadays Clancy Can't Even Sing' (Neil Young) b/w 'Go And Say Goodbye' (Stephen Stills)

This was chosen as the first single from the album and released in August 1966. For some unfathomable reason, it wasn't a huge hit and didn't even crack the Hot 100, hanging around at 110 on the charts.

'Burned' (Neil Young) b/w 'Everybody's Wrong' (Stephen Stills)

'Burned' was the second track lifted from the album and released in November 1966. Again, it was a sound that seemed chart-friendly but did even worse than the first single.

'For What It's Worth (Stop, Hey What's That Sound)' (Stephen Stills) b/w 'Do I Have To Come Right Out And Say It' (Neil Young)

The third release was not featured on the album. The track was freshly recorded and produced from the outset as a single. Stephen wrote it following a trip to San Francisco, where they met up with Moby Grape. It was heavily influenced by two Grape songs: 'Murder In My Heart For The Judge' and 'On The Other Side'. The title for 'For What It's Worth' came about from an aside during a car journey with his manager Charley Green. Steve, in the back, picked up a guitar and said: 'Let me play you a new song, for what it's worth'. On completion, its chart potential was instantly recognised and the clear production maximised its commercial possibilities.

The Stephen Stills song content was based on the riots that had taken place on the Sunset Strip in 1966, a type of topical songwriting that had its roots in the folk tradition popularised by Dylan. The riots followed a clampdown by the police on the counterculture. The establishment was taking a very dim view of the 'hippie' culture, with its unconventional appearance, anti-establishment lifestyle, hedonism and liberal attitudes to sex and drug taking. They set about harassing the freaks in a very heavy-handed manner, battering heads with wooden batons and making many arrests. They brought in curfews and loitering laws that were aimed at closing down the West Hollywood scene. They made the Whiskey A Go Go change its name and ordered the closure and demolition of Pandor's Box, a favourite club. The result was that the counter-culture turned out in force to protest. The police became more violent and broke up peaceful demonstrations with excessive force, causing the situation to escalate into a series of ugly riots.

Stephen, in his lyrics, captured the tension, antipathy and suspicion caused by the establishment. They viewed the counterculture's antiwar, civil rights, liberal attitudes and anti-capitalist stance as a threat to the American way of life and set out to crush it. The music reflected the menace of the confrontation. What was unusual was his put-down of those members of the counterculture who had gone along to the demonstrations with the intention of provoking violence.

It's no surprise that the song was seized upon by young people as an anthem of the times. Despite its commercial sensibilities as a pop song, it still resonated with the underground counterculture. Buffalo Springfield were fully accepted as bona fide members of the new sixties scene.

The track opens with Still's stinging, piercing, bell-like lead guitar notes. The rhythm section set up a pounding beat as Young and Stills enter a guitar duel. Still's vocal comes in clear, well annunciated and very much to the fore. The opening line sets the tone – 'There's something happening here'. He goes on to refer to guns, threats, division and violence: 'Battle lines being drawn', 'paranoia strikes deep', 'Hooray for our side', 'Nobody's right if everybody's wrong', 'Young People speaking their minds are getting so much resistance from behind'. All strong stuff.

Stills is seeing that factions on both sides were angling for confrontation. The song was a warning not to play into the establishment's hands by using violence. The chorus, delivered with backing vocals from the band, has a chilling message: 'Stop children, what's that sound? Everybody look what's going down'.

While the song was very much a counter-culture number, like many other songs from bands like The Doors and Jefferson Airplane that hit the singles charts, it had a very distinctive, radio-friendly sound and a commercial appeal that propelled it into the Top Ten. The band found themselves thrust into the instant stardom that Neil alludes to in 'Out Of My Mind'.

Following the huge success of the single 'For What It's Worth (Stop, Hey What's That Sound)', the album was re-released in March 1967 with the single as the first track. They dropped 'Baby Don't Scold Me' and slightly readjusted the running order of the album.

Buffalo Springfield Again (1967)

Personnel:
Stephen Stills: vocals, guitars, keyboards
Neil Young: vocals, guitars
Richie Furay: vocals, rhythm guitar
Bruce Palmer: bass guitar
Dewey Martin: vocals, drums
James Burton: Dobro on 'A Child's Claim To Fame'
Chris Sarns: guitar on 'Broken Arrow'
Charlie Chin: banjo on 'Bluebird'
Jack Nitzsche: electric piano on 'Expecting To Fly'
Don Randi: piano on 'Expecting To Fly' and 'Broken Arrow'
Jim Fielder: bass on 'Everydays'
Bobby West: bass on 'Bluebird'
The American Soul Train: horn section on 'Good Time Boy'
Jim Horn: clarinet
Norris Badeaux: baritone saxophone
Doug Hastings, Russ Titelman: guitars
Carol Kaye: bass
Hal Blaine, Jim Gordon: drums
Merry Clayton, Patrice Holloway, Gloria Jones, Shirley Matthews, Harvey
Newmark, Gracia Nitzsche: backing vocals
Loring Eutemey: design
Eve Babitz: cover illustration
Producers: Richie Furay, Jack Nitzsche, Stephen Stills, Neil Young, Brian Stone,
Dewey Martin, Charles Greene, Ahmet Ertegun
Engineers: Bruce Botnick, Bill Lazarus, Jim Messina, Ross Myering
Recorded at Columbia Studios Hollywood, Sunset Sound L.A.
Label: Atco Records
Chart positions: US: 44

The recording of the second album was a much more fraught affair compared
to the first. The initial enthusiasm and camaraderie within the band had
broken down. Things had begun to fall apart, with lots of the usual show
biz shenanigans, which is why it took nine months to record. There were
problems with management, egos between band members, drug busts and
deportations and people coming and going. It is not the ideal basis for
producing a work of art. On top of that, Neil was in a mess with his health.
He'd started having regular seizures, which were scaring the life out of him
and making him even more distant and withdrawn. The constant put-downs
from Stephen were messing with his confidence. The pressure was telling.

To start with, and most critically, Bruce Palmer was arrested on a drug
offence and deported. Although he came back illegally to record with the
band on a few tracks, some session men had to be used on others. That left a

hole in the chemistry of the band; Bruce's funky bass was a major ingredient and his personality was part of the glue.

Neil Young left and returned a few times. One of his absences was at the prestigious Monterey Pop Festival, where Stills got David Crosby to fill in for him. Neil actually recorded the song 'Expecting To Fly' with session musicians; Jack Nitzsche thought it was going to be for his first solo album but found that it was, in fact, going to be included on the Buffalo Springfield album. Nobody else from Buffalo Springfield appears on the track.

Neil Young had left the band for good for the second time but came back while actually heading for the airport when he heard 'Mr Soul' being played on the radio. It made him realise just how great they were together. He brought three brilliant tracks with him that he had recorded for a solo album he had in mind. The others overdubbed vocals and instruments onto his tracks and he overdubbed guitar on what they had produced. The Neil Young solo tracks metamorphosised into Buffalo Springfield tracks.

By now, the three main players were barely interacting or even talking to each other. Each recorded their own songs for the other band members or session men to come and overdub their parts. Incredibly, it all held together and retained a Buffalo Springfield flavour, and as a consequence, there are some exceptional songs on the record.

One final interesting detail is that the album no longer relied on Stephen and Neil to do all the songwriting and featured a few Richie Furay songs – laying the foundation for his work with his future band Poco, which would be formed following the demise of Buffalo Springfield.

All in all, the album itself is a patchwork rather than a unified creation from a tight band, but it is also clearly a progression. The musicians had grown in varying ways and developed a wider range of interests. There is a move away from the simpler guitar-based folk-rock sound of the first album into a richer panoply of sounds and genres. Richie had become more confident in his singing and had upgraded his songwriting. He was cultivating a distinctive country music flavour. Neil was becoming more psychedelic and avante garde and Stephen was developing his more commercial bluesy pop-rock style. Along with an underlying jazz influence, each of the members had headed off in very different directions. While the album was a conglomeration of solo projects, it still hangs together due to the brilliance of the musicianship and songwriting. Thus, *Buffalo Springfield Again* provides us with an array of instrumentation and experimentation involving a more interesting variety of styles.

The cover design by Loring Eutemey, using an illustration by Eve Babitz, is rather strange: a headland with trees, a strange fair-haired goddess in blue robes, a butterfly, a giant bluebird and a gallery of the band members, with folded arms, levitating above the sea below like gods presiding over some paradise, all bordered with flowers.

'Mr. Soul' (Neil Young)
The album kicks off with probably its second most outstanding track. This
is a Neil Young tour de force. Neil takes the lead vocal, amply backed up
by Stephen and Richie, with Stephen also supplying superb, free-flowing,
psychedelic guitar. For the first time, Neil is using a double drop D tuning,
to play a riff that is ripped off from the Stones' 'I Can't Get No Satisfaction'.
The rhythm section sets up a relentless rhythm that really motors, a pace
that is heightened by Neil's superb, highly original raucous guitar work.
Then Stephen comes in with a burst of scintillating strident guitar. The guitar
interaction in the middle eight is complex and inventive, with some fuzz
effects thrown in, creating a psychedelic touch. This type of spontaneous,
intricate guitar work characterised the brilliance of Stephen and Neil's
intuitive jousting and is the hallmark of their work. They gel to bring out the
best in each other.

Neil's obscure lyrics are also teasingly brilliant. It seems that Neil is already
sick of being a performing seal in this travelling circus of a pop band. He is
not sure about the screaming fans and the part he is playing in this band as
the weird one: 'She said, 'You're strange, but don't change, and I let her'. He's
fed up with having to play this part: 'Stick around while the clown who is
sick does the trick of disaster'. In many ways, the track documents the demise
of the band.

'A Child's Claim To Fame' (Richie Furay)
Richie takes the lead vocal on his own song backed by James Burton (who
first played as a 15-year-old on Dale Hawkins' 'Suzie Q' and went on to play
in Elvis's band) playing Dobro (a wooden-bodied resonator guitar). The
number has that Poco-style country rock feel. The double-tracked vocals
give it real power and there are some incredible interactions between James
Burton's intricate slide-guitar on the dobro and Richie's plucked strings.

The lyrics, which could be interpreted as being aimed at a girl, are actually
directed at Neil Young, who frustratingly keeps leaving and rejoining the
band, and reflect Richie's annoyance and frustration with Neil's behaviour. It
seems that Neil did not catch on to this until the 2011 reunion tour.

'Everydays' (Stephen Stills)
This track was recorded while Bruce Palmer had been deported back to
Canada on drug offences, and so Jim Fielder (from Blood Sweat & Tears)
steps in on bass. It is a Stephen Stills number with Stephen taking the lead
vocal. Stephen creates a different mood on this experimental number, with its
sultry, jazzy feel. His soft voice is exceedingly mellow with bluesy overtones.
It starts on an extended note, with some slow tinkling piano, before some
protracted E-string feedback from Neil, which is like a sustained organ note,
creates a drone that extends throughout. The effect supposedly occurred
accidentally in the studio, but they liked it enough to retain it throughout

the track. The song continues with a jazz-infused bubbling bass and the odd bursts of fuzz guitar, fading away with some shaking of beads and the organ note wavering out to create an extraordinary and highly original piece.

Stephen's poetic, mystical lyrics about life passing us by are crooned over the top of this jazzy backing to create a warm ambience. 'Like ecstasy, the sound of trees. Most anything, what a baby sees'. The message is clear – we need to get going and appreciate the world around us: 'Drive over hills, forget your fear. Getting it out of second gear'.

'Expecting To Fly' (Neil Young)

This is a solo masterpiece by Neil and probably the most ambitious and successful track on the album. It clearly shows why the band were prepared to put up with Neil's bullshit and health problems and kept accepting him back. It was worth it when he came up with gems like this. It's a track full of innovation that was masterly arranged by the late great Jack Nitzsche. The song was actually produced before the advent of *Sgt. Pepper*, but clearly demonstrates the same enormity of ambition.

Neil, during one of his absences from the band, actually thought he was recording the track for his planned solo album, but went back to Buffalo Springfield and took the track with him – thus, it was included on the album. The song was recorded without any members of Buffalo Springfield but with the superb, seasoned session musicians known as The Wrecking Crew, a group of musicians used extensively in the Los Angeles studios, who appeared on hundreds of Top 40 hits. Neil and Jack worked on it solidly for 30 days straight.

Jack's arrangements and use of strings and oboe took the track to new heights not heard before. The way he melded the various segments and components together to form an epic song made up of seemingly unrelated elements was quite unique The orchestration adds another dimension to help hold it together perfectly and help transform the song into an ethereal masterpiece. Later, Richie Furay overdubbed his rich vocals onto it, which blend beautifully with Neil's voice to create something even more special.

The track starts with an orchestral build that is reminiscent of The Beatles' 'A Day In The Life', except that it doesn't crash; instead, it melts into an amazingly atmospheric piece of orchestration. Neil's wraithlike vocals and guitar are eerie and supernatural, with sobbing strings and guitar creating a soft, haunting melody. The track is unique, with its transcendental, mystical mood. Persevering with Neil despite his unreliability certainly paid off.

The lyrics are a lament to a past love, Neil's first experience of shy love-making, so sensual and sad – a nostalgic opus to loss and possibility.

'Bluebird' (Stills)

Bruce Palmer was also absent for this one. Bobby West stood in on bass. Stephen also had Charlie Chin on banjo for the last part of the song. This is a love song for Stephen's flighty, blue-eyed lover Judy Collins. Their relationship was always difficult, with her not wishing to be tied down. In the end, she flew away; Stephen likens her to a beautiful bluebird.

The busted Palmer was in Canada and Neil had left. At the time, it looked as if Buffalo Springfield were no more, but Stephen laid the track down as an acoustic guitar number, and when Neil rejoined, he overdubbed the electric guitar. It's a rockin' track with a searing lead intro from Neil. The blend of Stephen's elaborate acoustic guitars and Neil's mammoth electric overdubs works magnificently. Stephen's acoustic, a 1937 Martin D-28, was given the treatment in the studio, using compression, equaliser and limiters to enhance the sound so that it could compete with Neil's electric guitar. The result was a huge, metallic sound that chimed clearly to create the perfect sparring partner for Neil's free-form playing.

The rest of the band put in an equally effective performance. Dewey's steady drumbeat sets a fast pace and Bobby West provides a bass that throbs and then burbles along underneath like a flowing river. The falsetto voice section is exceptional as it adds a wraithlike quality. The last section of the track proceeds after a pause. It's much quieter, has a different time signature – more in the bluegrass style – and is based around acoustic guitar and banjo, creating a totally different feel to that of the rockier sections that preceded it. This multipart epic is certainly Stephen's outstanding track on the album.

The track was released in three very different versions. The two-minute edited single is more of a straight folk-rocker, the four-and-a-half-minute album track is what I am referring to here and there is also a nine-minute extended version of this number, with an amazing elongated instrumental section of dueling guitars. The extended version was released on the 1973 *Buffalo Springfield* compilation album.

'Hung Upside Down' (Stills)

Richie takes the lead vocals on this Stills classic. It seems that everything is getting to Stephen, probably Judy Collins leaving him, but also the disintegration of the band and the strange days of the late sixties, with the Vietnam War, civil rights assassinations, drugs and political unrest. Enough to hang anybody upside down. Stephen finds himself sitting up till three in the morning, confused and not seeing a way forward, feeling depressed and sorry for himself. When you're in that kind of mood, it usually makes for a great burst of creativity – as we see here.

The track starts with some strummed guitar from Stephen, with Neil providing an economy of more strident chords. Richie's vocals are warm and expressive, creating a mellow, melancholy mood. The song builds towards a storming instrumental section of interweaving guitars. Stephen provides backing vocals in the chorus. The song then thunders off into another instrumental passage, with some exceptional guitar work from Stephen. Richie's singing becomes more insistent and intense, with a hint of optimism, as the song builds towards an instrumental climax, finishing with the same Neil Young guitar riff.

'Sad Memory' (Furay)

This is a Richie Furay track, first recorded as a solo project, on which Richie takes the lead vocals and plays acoustic guitar, with Neil providing some overdubbed lead guitar. The rest of the band does not feature at all. The track is a nostalgic love song delivered poignantly by Richie, with a simple acoustic guitar accompaniment. The piece starts with a slow strum across the strings, which sets the mood. Richie's voice is gently lilting, so full of sadness and regret, as he looks back at the idyll of the past and a lost love.

Neil's electric guitar suits the track effectively, beautifully crafted as a soft, ethereal series of notes, kept in the background and unobtrusively adding to the mood.

'Good Time Boy' (Furay)

This is a rarity as Dewey takes the lead vocal on this Richie Furay number. His raspy voice lacks the warmth of Richie's, the unique quirkiness of Neil's or the power of Stephen's, but it seems to suit this up-tempo, good-time song. It's a complete change of mood from the previous emotionally charged track. Forget the lilting – this track bounces along, raucous and loud, complete with an R&B brass section reminiscent of Blood, Sweat & Tears. It rocks. The brass section comes courtesy of the Memphis Horns. It's uncertain if Dewey also plays drums on the track or whether that was one of the session men. Otherwise, he restricts himself to the vocals. In terms of subject matter, it's rather straightforward: Dewey claims to be a good-time man and that's about it. He's never going to be true. Get used to it.

'Rock & Roll Woman' (Stills, Crosby)

Stephen wrote this with David Crosby. Stephen takes the lead and David can just about be heard on backing vocals with the rest of the band. The song is an ode to the great Grace Slick of Jefferson Airplane. She's a real rock 'n' roll woman.

In many ways, it is the track which is most reminiscent of the first album, starting with a repeating acoustic guitar refrain that is then picked up by the backing vocals. Stills' powerful, soulful voice performs the eulogy; the wonder of that voice is clearly heard when the instruments drop out, leaving the rest of the band to provide layers of harmony. Apart from Stephen's guitar, there are contributions from Doug Hastings and I'm sure that Neil's more strident tremolo guitar is also in there.

The acoustic section is very busy. The amazing bass line lays down a meaty foundation and, appropriately for the subject matter, it builds to a rocky conclusion, with organ filling out the sound and a catchy backing vocal chorus. I bet Grace Slick was suitably chuffed.

'Broken Arrow' (Young)

Neil has crammed so much into this six-minute epic, a surreal medley of sections pasted together with enigmatic, cinema-esque trickery. The plaintive vocal and melancholy music draws out the emotions in this tapestry of evocative metaphors.

The piece seems to chart the history of America, from the plight of the Native Americans to the assassination of JFK. One can peel away the layers. It begins with Neil's own disillusionment with fame and proceeds to identify with the plight of the Native American Indians; their genocide, the loss of hope and the emptiness that is left. 'Did you see them?' The lone Indian with the empty quiver and broken arrow – that lone Indian represents all of his people and the way of life that is lost. The song relates that to the emptiness of fame. It takes us to the loss of hope with the death of JFK. Even so, the words are poetically obscure enough to allow many interpretations – all equally valid.

The song was dedicated to Ken Koblun as a form of atonement. Ken was a friend of Neil's from the days of The Squires. He had found some success with a Canadian band called 3s A Crowd. When Bruce got himself busted and was deported, they looked around for a replacement and Ken was persuaded to leave 3s A Crowd to join Buffalo Springfield. Ken thought that it was a permanent move, but the band only saw him as a temporary replacement. He was later dumped, having burnt his bridges and left in the lurch. Neil felt very guilty. A broken arrow is a symbol of peace after war. Maybe this is a symbol of Neil's guilt concerning what they had done to Ken. Or maybe, going back to the subject of America, that broken arrow symbolises the destruction of the entire Native American nation and the loss of their way of life.

The epic was produced by Jack Nitzsche and is a work of genius. He took the disparate elements and melded the sections together with snippets of sound to make a bizarre sequence of thought-provoking music. Thus, it was something more than a song – it became a collage of sound made up of discrete sections of music.

It starts with a slab of 'Mr. Soul' being played live in front of a barrage of screams (actually taken from a Beatles concert). This then segues into, what sounds like, an orchestral opening as the tonic is sustained, before marching drums lead into the first verse, with the words delivered in a melancholy manner (the reference to a black limo in the first verse could be a hearse (Mort?)). The show's over; no more screams. They are left with the emptiness – the reality.

The beat picks up for the chorus. 'Did you see them?' The Indian stands on the banks of the river, his quiver empty, holding a broken arrow. The chorus segues into crowd noise before a brief section of circus organ, which then wavers into the next verse – a verse about families, loss, a brother, perhaps a casualty of Vietnam.

The chorus gallops back in with strings, then military drums and into the third verse. The one of Kings and Queens: JFK? And the loss of that dream?

'They married for peace and were gone'. As the chorus – with its strings – fades away, the piece segues into a jazzy section with clarinet and ends with a piano solo from Don Randi.

One is left with a number of thoughts and feelings wafting around in one's head, as if the meaning was all there but not fully conscious, beyond analysis, beyond being nailed down to any one interpretation.

In a number of ways, it reminds me of The Beatles' 'A Day In The Life' in the way it moves through the different moods and separate, distinct sections, although the vibe is different to that of The Beatles and that Beatles track had not been released until Neil's had already been recorded.

Singles
'Bluebird' b/w 'Mr Soul'
The album was not released until the end of October 1967, but this single was put out in June as a double-sided taster. For some obscure reason, in an attempt to gain more radio play, 'Bluebird' was edited down to 1:59 – probably an attempt to align it with the musical style of the first album. Despite its obvious quality, the single failed to do as well as expected, only making the fifties in the charts.

'Rock And Roll Woman' b/w 'A Child's Claim To Fame'
This single, lifted straight off the album, was released in September 1967 and did a little better, rising to the low forties in the charts.

'Expecting To Fly' b/w 'Everydays'
This, too, was lifted from the album and released in December 1967, a couple of months after the album had been released. It only just crept into the hot hundred at number 98.

Conclusion
The album was over. Despite the more disparate elements, the solo ventures, different musicians, lack of unity of the group and absence of cohesion, it still very much felt like a Buffalo Springfield album and the quality held up, perhaps even exceeding that of the first album.

Last Time Around (1968)

Personnel:

Richie Furay: guitar (1, 2, 3, 8, 10, 11, 12), vocals (1, 2, 3, 5, 7, 10, 12)

Dewey Martin: drums (1, 2, 3, 9, 11)

Jim Messina: bass, vocals (5, 12)

Stephen Stills: guitar (1, 2, 3, 4, 6, 8, 10, 11), piano (4, 6, 8), B3 organ (6, 8, 11), bass (6, 8), clavinet (8), vibes (1), percussion (11), handclaps (11), background vocal (1, 5, 8, 10), lead vocal (3, 4, 6, 8, 11)

Neil Young: guitar (3, 9, 10), harmonica (9), piano (1), background vocal (1), lead vocal (9)

Bruce Palmer: bass (1)

Jim Fielder: bass (3)

Buddy Miles: drums (6)

Jimmy Karstein: drums (8, 10)

Gary Marker: bass (9)

Jeremy Stuart: harpsichord, calliope, bells (10)

Rusty Young: pedal steel guitar (12)

Richard Davis: bass (12)

Unidentified: horns (1), saxophone, clarinet (2), drums (4), bass, drums, harpsichord, orchestra (7), horn (11), piano, drums (12)

Producer: Jim Messina

Recorded at Sunset Sound, Los Angeles, California, Sound Recorders, Hollywood and Atlantic Studios, New York City

Label: Atco Records

Chart positions: US: 42

This was nothing more than a mish-mash of tracks thrown together in order to meet the band's contractual obligations. The band had disintegrated. The various members were much more concerned with their new enterprises than pouring any of their precious creativity into this dead duck. Stills was delighting in the early days of Crosby, Stills & Nash, writing songs and fooling around in Laurel Canyon, perfecting their harmonies in loose acoustic jams in various sitting rooms. Young was working on solo projects and was in the early stages of jamming with the local band, The Rockets, who would later become Crazy Horse. Furay was working with Jim Messina and Rusty York to put together Poco. Palmer was still banished from the States and suffering from legal restrictions that prevented him from working (at one point, he was going to work with Crosby, Stills & Nash but was prevented).

With contractual obligations providing the necessity, Richie and Jim Messina cobbled the album together. Fortunately, there were a lot of unreleased songs, so they were able to assemble the album mainly from material that had been recorded previously without the need to reassemble the team. Probably, because of this, the album was imbued with more of a soft country vibe in contrast to the previous album. Jim Messina took on the role of producing the album, as well as most of the bass work. Bruce Palmer only played on one track and the whole band only appeared together on one track (Neil's 'On the Way Home').

Surprisingly, despite the album's lacklustre process of creation, it was by no means a throw-away album. The songwriters contributed material that, while being part of their 'old' longstanding repertoire, was far from substandard. Hence, the album tended to receive good reviews.

Interestingly, the cover artwork was rather appropriately put together from individual shots of the members of the band pasted together. It features all the band members in profile facing one way, except for Neil Young, who is facing in the opposite direction.

'On The Way Home' (Young)

This song had been a staple in Neil's live performances for a long time, and once again, he shares vocals with Richie, though Richie is the main vocalist and Neil is relegated to support. It is the only time on the album that the band are all together and the only track that Bruce Palmer plays on. Richie's vocal rendition gives it a lighter, faster production than Neil's versions. The guitar sounds higher in pitch.

The song itself has many interpretations. Firstly, one can deduct from the lyrics that it's a marijuana song: 'I held my breath with my eyes closed. I went insane, like a smoke ring day when the wind blows'. Secondly, many have interpreted the lyrics as being about Neil's departure from Buffalo Springfield. Lastly, it is about leaving a girl behind in his wake. Probably all three.

Moby Grape's Peter Lewis said, 'Maybe 'On The Way Home' was the coolest rock song written during that period'. Stills has always claimed that it was written for him.

It would later appear on Crosby, Stills, Nash & Young's *4-Way Street* live album.

'It's So Hard To Wait' (Furay, Young)

A really unusual jazz piece from Richie. His smooth, rich voice has the perfect late-night feel. Shuffling drums, lazy groans from the bass, slow tempo, bluesy horn. Not Richie's usual country style at all, but he handles it magnificently. The vocal is glorious, so full of emotion and nuance – an achingly beautiful love song. Neil shares the writing credits for this piece, but I can't detect his influence anywhere.

'Pretty Girl Why' (Stills)

This number also has a jazzy feel but with a much faster tempo. Dewey sets a crisp beat and Jim Fielder lays down a bass that throbs like a heartbeat throughout the track. The gentle guitar blends with Stephen's warm, lilting voice to create a perfect love song. The poetic lyrics, the consummate interplay of the instruments and the haunting melody are all testaments to what superb musicians and songwriters they were. Another ode to the wayward Judy Collins? Or, as some have reported, a song for the actress Nancy Priddy?

'Four Days Gone' (Stills)
An antiwar song with a difference, as Stephen relates the tale of a guy absconding from the 'military madness' of the call-up to fight in Vietnam. He's four days on the run, hitching back to pick up his baby and flee, meeting kindness and understanding while on the road, but also an implied unpleasantness – 'I met two kinds of people on the road'. Stephen's mellow vocal carries great sorrow and emotion as he tells the story in this piano-based number. Crisp, steady drums and slow, meandering bass, along with some spread-out slashing guitar chords (which sound like Neil), simmer in the background. Stephen's guitar playing is immaculate, as usual.

'Carefree Country Day' (Messina)
Jim Messina emerges from behind the mixing desk to present us with one of his own compositions. This laid-back country ditty – a song of contentment in the country idyll – with jazz overtones and even a bit of scat singing at the end, doesn't have any of the Buffalo Springfield trademark vocal, harmony or instrumental characteristics at all. It doesn't sound a bit like Buffalo Springfield in the least. Pleasant enough, I suppose.

'Special Care' (Stills)
This is pretty much a Stephen Stills solo effort. He plays guitars, B3 Hammond organ, pianos and bass, with Buddy Miles on drums. That firm drumbeat is the foundation. Stephen does a great job on the bass; it rambles and burbles brilliantly and that Hammond B3 organ is a blast. Apart from that, there are all the Stills hallmarks: the terrific expressive vocal and superb guitar solos, with extended notes as clear as laser rays.

It seems that people have been taking Stephen for a fool, someone who is past it that they are trying to bring down – 'Do you think I'm blowing my cool, playing the fool? Do you think I'm someone gone? Would you like to shoot me down?' Well, you don't mess with Stephen. He's past caring, he's got nothing to lose and he'll blow you to bits: 'To make you aware I've been forsaken and if you don't care, there's a bomb to blow your house down, Oh yeah'.

'The Hour Of Not Quite Rain' (Micki Callen, Furay)
This track is a peculiarity. The band had somehow gotten themselves involved with a competition run by a local LA radio station called KHJ. The radio station wanted listeners to send in their poetry, the prize being that Buffalo Springfield would put music to the winner's poem and record it. I don't know how the band felt about that, but they must have agreed to it in the first place. One Micki Callen won $1000, plus publishing royalties, and the band, honouring their promise, recorded this track.

Sung by Richie Furay, he captures the surreal, ethereal qualities of the poem by using an orchestral arrangement. The violins, cellos and flutes meld with Richie's strained, mystical, floating vocal to create an eerie feel. The drums lurch through as the magic of the production plays with the spooky images. It works.

'Questions' (Stills)

Another showcase for Stephen Stills and his multi-talented skills as a musician. He's a one-man band – well, two-man actually, with Jimmy Karstein on drums. Stephen's bass playing is immaculate and dominates the piece with some intricate melodic patterns. Right from the 12-string intro, the song launches into a feast of instrumentation. Jimmy Karstein's drums, while being a little clunky, provide a steady platform for Stephen to layer his range of other instruments: Hohner clavinet, bass, guitars – is there no end to his skills? The guitar playing is, as always, exceptional. The fuzz overtones in the instrumental passage are the result of a rewound pick-up on the guitar, not a pedal. Come on, girl – tell him all about yourself. He wants to know everything. His head is full of questions.

My one criticism is that the production is not bright enough and fails to provide the separation to give the instrumentation greater clarity. A verse of this song was later grafted onto Crosby, Stills, Nash & Young's 'Carry On/Questions' on *Déjà Vu* and I much prefer the crispness of that production.

No sign of Neil on this track. I don't think he's there.

'I Am A Child' (Young)

An early track that featured regularly in Neil's live act, this celebrates childhood and captures its innocence, while also highlighting the two-way process of learning and joy. It suggests Neil is trying hard to hang on to that innocence and openness. Neil has stated that in no way was it a response to Richie's veiled attack on him and his cantankerous ways in the track 'A Child's Claim To Fame'.

He recorded this version as a solo effort. The only member of Buffalo Springfield who appears on it is Dewey Martin, the drummer. The bass was played by Gary Marker. This is actually the only track on the album where Neil sings lead vocals. The vocal is extremely soft and out of character – so mellow and controlled for Neil. Other versions that he did have a harsher sound. The harmonica break is very Neil-like, though, the intricate acoustic guitars give the track a distinct Buffalo Springfield feel, even if they are all Neil's work, and neither Stills nor Furay added to it. Dewey's drums are very prominent throughout.

'Merry-Go-Round' (Furay)

A fairly inconsequential, lightweight solo effort from Richie Furay, with Jimmy Karstein on drums and bass and Jeremy Stuart providing the fairground bells, harpsichord and calliope.

I find it to be a love song without a great deal of substance. The instrumentation creates a circular refrain that is light and airy, evoking the swirl of the fairground. The bass gives this lightweight track a little body. She's got him up and down with his feet off the ground like on a fairground ride. Doesn't do much for me.

'Uno Mundo' (Stills)
This is Stills' early stab at world music, with an infectious Latin beat. Although he has Richie Furay on guitar and Dewey on drums, this is another opportunity for Stephen to show off his amazing versatility and musicianship. He not only takes lead vocal, lead guitar and rhythm guitar but also handles the Hammond B3 organ and impressive Brazilian Samba percussion, and that's probably him on bass, too. There's no end to the man's abilities. He's manic. Despite the message that things around the world need fixing, the number has an upbeat feel, with the Samba drums and bongos overlaid with Stephen's smooth, seamless, fluid guitar. Even Stephen's vocals are perky.

'Uno mundo, Asia is screaming. Uno mundo, Africa's seething. Uno mundo, America bleating. Uno mundo, just the same'. We are all one people on one planet, coursing through the heavens together. When are we going to sort it out? 'Uno mundo, somos equals. Uno mundo, porque no ames' – 'One world we are equal. One world because of no love'. The message is straightforward and clear – the world is the way it is because we don't care enough.

'Kind Woman' (Furay)
A Richie Furay effort in what was another precursor to Poco, with a slow piano-based love song. He's joined by Rusty Young on pedal steel guitar and Richard Davis on bass. The drummer and pianist remain unknown, but it's nobody from Buffalo Springfield.

The song features Richie's smooth, silky voice, with Jim Messina on backing vocals. The drums are softly in the background and the bass carries it forward with a slow, uniform beat. Come on kind woman – give him some loving tonight. He's a lonely man.

Singles
'Uno Mundo' b/w **'Merry-Go-Round'**
This single was lifted straight off the album and failed to make the Hot Hundred, stalling at 105.

'Special Care' b/w 'Kind Woman'
Another single straight off the album fairing the same as the first, stalling at 107 in the Hot Hundred.

'On The Way Home' b/w 'Four Days Gone'
The third and last single from the album. It did a little better than the previous two, entering the Hot Hundred and reaching number 82.

Buffalo Springfield Compilations

Retrospective: The Best Of Buffalo Springfield (1969)

Retrospective does what it sets out to do: it brings together all the best songs, the most commercial songs, from the three albums. Opening with the obvious, evocative 'For What It's Worth', it progresses through a range of their best tracks. From Neil, there is the high tempo 'Mr Soul', the rebellious 'Nowadays Clancy Can't Even Sing', the epic multi-layered 'Broken Arrow', the wonderful 'Expecting To Fly' and the plaintive 'I Am A Child'. These are augmented with 'Sit Down I Think I Love You', 'Kind Woman', 'Bluebird', 'On The Way Home', 'Rock & Roll Woman' and 'Go And Say Goodbye'.

For me, it reinforces the view that Neil was the superior songwriter, but also fails as a 'Best of' because it does not include some of the more subtle and less commercial numbers that were among their best – such as 'Everydays', 'Burned' and 'Flying On The Ground Is Wrong'.

Overall, it fails to give a balanced view of the talents of the band. It's too in your face with too little of the subtlety.

Buffalo Springfield (1973)

For me, this does a better job of being a 'Best of'. That's mainly because, as a double album with far more tracks, it gives a wider picture of their talents, styles and subtleties. This is more what the band really were. The album is more balanced, containing not just the numbers that instantly scream at you but some of the more nuanced numbers as well. Apart from anything else, it is worth getting just for the nine-minute version of 'Bluebird'.

The track listing tells the story: 'For What It's Worth', 'Sit Down I Think I Love You', 'Nowadays Clancy Can't Even Sing', 'Pay The Price', 'Burned', 'Out Of My Mind', 'Mr Soul', 'Bluebird' (nine-minute version with duelling guitar jam), 'Broken Arrow', 'Rock 'n' Roll Woman', 'Expecting To Fly', 'Hung Upside Down', 'Special Care', 'Uno Mundo', 'A Child's Claim To Fame', 'Kind Woman', 'On The Way Home', 'I Am A Child', 'Pretty Girl Why?', 'In The Hour Of Not Quite Rain', 'Four Days Gone' and 'Questions'.

Buffalo Springfield (box set) (2001)

This was the lavish box set that appeared to have it all and very nearly did. While it offered the earth, with an abundance of rare tracks, demos and unreleased material, it tantalisingly failed to deliver everything it could have done. There is duplication and numerous omissions.

One mustn't complain. With four CDs of Springfield material, including 36 previously unreleased tracks, all with excellent remastering from the original analogue master tapes, there is not a lot to complain about. The sound is exceptional. And it comes with a detailed 68-page booklet!

The box set presents a dilemma. As the book is about Neil Young and not Buffalo Springfield per se, there is the question of whether to include the tracks that Neil has no input on. I am therefore only focussing on the tracks on which Neil performed, although all tracks are listed.

The tracks are ordered according to their recording date.

Disc 1

Disc one is a treasure trove of new material, consisting of 12 unreleased demos, the remasters of the tracks from *Buffalo Springfield* and one unreleased track featuring the whole band. There are some worthy Neil Young rarities that I will highlight:

'There Goes My Baby' is a previously unreleased demo for Sonny & Cher, produced by Neil's then-managers Brian Stone and Charles Green, who wanted to hawk the song to Sonny and Cher. This is a stark performance, with Neil on a slowly strummed acoustic guitar.

A simple song of lost love, the slow, chiming guitar provides a funereal sadness. Neil's voice expresses the sadness well. A very different vibe to the Doo-Wop-ish production with Comrie Smith.

'Out Of My Mind' is what the song sounded like with just an acoustic strummed guitar and some rudimentary backing vocals, prior to it being adorned with that Leslie-fed guitar and the lavish harmonies that transformed it into a psychedelic gem. It's not surprising that they kept Neil as the vocalist on the studio band version, as the required power and intensity is apparent on this demo. Neil, who forgets the lyrics towards the end and da-da's his way through, really carries the melody well. It always seems strange to me that Neil is singing about the strains of the music business, screaming fans and limousines, being controlled and the pressures driving him out of his mind before they've even made it big. This was a demo for the first album, before they hit the big time.

'Flying On The Ground Is Wrong' is another sparse solo demo. This is wonderful. To hear one of Neil's epic songs bereft of all adornment – just Neil and a roughly strummed acoustic. The melody is even stronger and the emotion is there. It works well in this basic format.

'I'm Your Kind Of Guy' goes from the sublime to something else entirely. This jaunty little fragment (just over a minute) sounds like an early sixties pop song by the likes of Del Shannon. It's very light and derivative.

'Down Down Down' is a revelation and a beautiful song, starting with some interesting acoustic guitar patterns, with Neil's voice sounding delicate and relaxed in a manner that I have rarely heard – so haunting and evocative. The lyrics are typical of Neil's oblique poetry. The girl has betrayed him and is begging for forgiveness (being down in the river desiring to be born again and renewed) and desiring repentance, as Neil suffers a heartrending struggle to forgive. He still needs her but he cannot trust her, yet he is guilty of the same infidelity. The song itself is a precursor of both Neil's later 'Broken Arrow' and Crosby, Stills, Nash & Young's 'Country Girl', but it stands very well on its own.

'Neighbor Don't You Worry' is a Stephen Stills number but this is the full-band version. They give it full treatment, with some great electric guitar work from Neil that creates a psychedelic sound.

Tracklisting:
1. 'There Goes My Babe' (Neil Young) – previously unreleased demo for Sonny & Cher
2. 'Come On' (Stephen Stills) – previously unreleased demo
3. 'Hello, I've Returned' (Stephen Stills/Van Dyke Parks) – previously unreleased demo
4. 'Out Of My Mind' (Neil Young) – previously unreleased demo
5. 'Flying On The Ground Is Wrong' (Neil Young) – previously unreleased demo
6. 'I'm Your Kind Of Guy (Neil Young)' – previously unreleased demo
7. 'Baby Don't Scold Me (Stephen Stills)' – previously unreleased demo
8. 'Neighbor Don't You Worry' (Stephen Stills) – previously unreleased demo
9. 'We'll See' (Stephen Stills) – previously unreleased demo
10. 'Sad Memory' (Richie Furay) – previously unreleased demo
11. 'Can't Keep Me Down' (Richie Furay) – previously unreleased demo
12. 'Nowadays Clancy Can't Even Sing' (Neil Young) – remaster of the track from *Buffalo Springfield*
13. 'Go And Say Goodbye' (Stephen Stills) – remaster of the track from *Buffalo Springfield*
14. 'Sit Down I Think I Love You' (Stephen Stills) – remaster of the track from *Buffalo Springfield*
15. 'Leave' (Stephen Stills) – remaster of the track from *Buffalo Springfield*
16. 'Hot Dusty Roads' (Stephen Stills) – remaster of the track from *Buffalo Springfield*
17. 'Everybody's Wrong' (Stephen Stills) – remaster of the track from *Buffalo Springfield*
18. 'Burned' (Neil Young) – remaster of the track from *Buffalo Springfield*
19. 'Do I Have To Come Right Out And Say It' (Neil Young) – remaster of the track from *Buffalo Springfield*
20. 'Out Of My Mind' (Neil Young) – remaster of the track from *Buffalo Springfield*
21. 'Pay The Price' (Stephen Stills) – remaster of the track from *Buffalo Springfield*
22. 'Down Down Down' (Neil Young) – previously unreleased demo
23. 'Flying On The Ground Is Wrong' (Neil Young) – remaster of the track from *Buffalo Springfield*
24. 'Neighbor Don't You Worry' (Stephen Stills) – previously unreleased

Disc 2
Disc two continues the fabulous work of uncovering brilliant gems that have been left neglected in the vaults. There are no less than eight wonderful unreleased full-band numbers, two whole-band studio jams, five previously

unreleased demos from Richie and Stephen and five remastered Buffalo Springfield tracks from the mono mix of *Buffalo Springfield Again*. It includes a plethora of Neil's songs.

'Down Down Down' is a Neil Young song given the full band treatment. It's great to hear what the full band have done to the song. It is completely different to Neil's demo. This is probably the greatest unreleased gem from the whole box set. It sets off as it means to go on, with the most beautiful electric guitar runs over Still's strumming. The way Neil and Stephen interact is always special; here, it is delicate and exquisite. The song progresses with the familiar melody of 'Broken Arrow' with those characteristic flowing harmonies. To hear Stills and Furay singing together is the essence of Buffalo Springfield for me. They've taken Neil's incredible solo demo and transformed it into a more complex masterpiece of different sections, including a line of spoken word. Why this remained unreleased is beyond me.

'Kahuna Sunset' – well, I thought I'd heard everything, but Buffalo Springfield trying their hand at doing a Hawaiian instrumental? Sounds pretty lightweight to me. I don't really like it. Perhaps the boys were just having fun jamming in the studio. Or is this Neil returning to his roots with The Squires and early sixties surf instrumentals? All members of the band were there on this one, with the addition of Hawaiian Cyrus Faryar on Hawaiian-style percussion. They certainly capture the Hawaiian sound, from the drum, bass and acoustic foundation to the slide and twangy guitars. It's even got some rather cheesy lapping waves. It slips into more of a surf sound towards the end, with some twangy guitar following some twiddling. But... Buffalo Springfield it isn't.

'Buffalo Stomp (Raga)' – a driving instrumental full of energy and spark. Dewey's pacey drumming combines with Bruce's solid bass to provide a pounding platform for the others to work off. Stephen and Richie's duelling guitars set up some great interweaving patterns and Neil's guitar comes in with real bite. It's even got Skip Spence (from Quicksilver Messenger Service/ Jefferson Airplane/Moby Grape) on kazoo to provide that drone. They called it a raga because it does have that Indian lilt and drone that gives it the flavour of a raga. But it also has that psychedelic flourish, with plenty of feedback, ending with a storm of shrieking guitar. They sure must have had fun jamming this in the studio.

'Baby Don't Scold' is the Stephen Stills number given the full band treatment. What a cracking version this is – far better than the earlier released track. Neil's fuzzed-up Leslie guitar adds a psychedelic feel. Richie and Steve's gymnastic harmonies gel superbly and bring out the melody. The three guitars merge together in the superb guitar section, in which, at the start, Neil slips in a little coda of The Beatles' 'Daytripper'. As they near the end, the whole band is flying, building to a crescendo. Superb!

'Mr. Soul' is one of the few disappointments. This sounds like a muddier version of a great song when compared to the released version. I much prefer the original, which sounds sharper and more intense to me.

'We'll See' is another Stephen Stills number given the full band treatment and makes its first appearance here. Another complete mystery. Why was this superb song never released at the time? It's brilliant. What a job the band did on what was already a delightful demo. Bruce's funky bass really pushes the song forward, with Dewey's dynamic drumming providing hyperdrive. Steve's vocal is superb and Richie provides a powerful boost. The two of them blend so brilliantly. Then we have Neil's smoking guitar riffs, with a touch of 'Mr Soul' thrown into the mix. This is vintage Buffalo Springfield. Anybody who thought that these tracks might prove to be lesser, lightweight songs would soon be put right when hearing gems like this.

'My Kind Of Love' is a Richie Furay song featuring the whole Buffalo Springfield and is an unreleased belter. This number sets off at a rollicking pace, Dewey's drums belting along and Bruce's bass as funky as hell. The acoustics set up a repeating riff for Richie's vocal to simply pour over. Another brilliant unearthed gem.

'Pretty Girl Why' takes the mood into a different dimension with this great version of the Stills song. The gentle production from Ahmet Ertegun gives the piece a jazzy, Latin flavour that is delightfully pleasant on the ear – at times, it's almost 'The Girl From Ipanema'. But he gets away with it. Stephen's voice is at its most lilting and the understated harmonising with Richie is sublime. Their voices meld together like honey and treacle. Dewey's drumming immaculately holds the piece together, with Jim Fielder capably handling the killer bass in the absence of Bruce Palmer. The reverse reverb on the cymbals adds a very distinctive sound. As with the luscious vocals, the guitars blend magnificently with Neil's, offering a contrast, as usual, with that use of distortion and echo. It doesn't get much more beautiful than this.

'No Sun Today' is the other letdown and is the only song written by the producer Eric Eisner. Despite having all the Buffalo Springfield ingredients (sadly, no Bruce Palmer – Jim Fielder takes his place), it doesn't do it for me. This sounds too much like a pedestrian sixties pop song. Nothing stands out and the usually superb interactions all sound a trifle off.

After the previous disappointment, we're back to another great discovery with 'Down To The Wire'. This is the version with Stephen Stills taking the vocals. The Neil Young vocal version was released on the *Decade* album in 1976. This version is quite different to the one in which Neil takes the lead. This is more psychedelic, yet sounds smoother. The number revolves around that chunky guitar riff, with Dewey's heavy drums augmented by percussion from Jesse Hill. Doctor John (Mac Rebennack) is supposedly playing some piano on this, but he's so far back in the mix that I can't hear him. He's more apparent on the Neil Young vocal take. The bass, with Bruce Palmer still missing, is handled by Bobby West. This version, because of Stephen's more lyrical singing and the more sophisticated production, is less raw and emotional than the Neil Young version, but it does feature some great psychedelic flourishes, as with the electric guitar solo played backwards to create a great waltz interlude a la The Beatles. Everybody is telling him that she's bad news. Things are heading for a showdown. She's a liar. But she still makes him hot and they were so good together. This was recorded for the abandoned *Stampede* album.

Tracklisting:
1. 'Down Down Down' (Neil Young) – previously unreleased
2. 'Kahuna Sunset' (Stephen Stills & Neil Young) – previously unreleased instrumental
3. 'Buffalo Stomp (Raga)' (Richie Furay, Bruce Kunkel, Dewey Martin, Stephen Stills & Neil Young) – previously unreleased instrumental
4. 'Baby Don't Scold Me' (Stephen Stills) – previously unreleased version
5. 'For What It's Worth' (Stephen Stills) – directly taken from *Buffalo Springfield*
6. 'Mr. Soul' (Neil Young) – previously unreleased version
7. 'We'll See' (Stephen Stills) – previously unreleased
8. 'My Kind Of Love' (Richie Furay) – previously unreleased
9. 'Pretty Girl Why' (Stephen Stills) – previously unreleased mix
10. 'Words I Must Say' (Richie Furay) – previously unreleased demo
11. 'Nobody's Fool' (Richie Fury song) – previously unreleased demo
12. 'So You've Got A Lover' (Stephen Stills) – previously unreleased demo
13. 'My Angel' (Stephen Stills) – previously unreleased demo
14. 'No Sun Today' (Eric Eisner) – previously unreleased
15. 'Everydays' (Stephen Stills) – from the mono mix of *Buffalo Springfield Again*
16. 'Down To The Wire' (Neil Young) – previously unreleased version
17. 'Bluebird' (Stephen Stills) – from the mono mix of *Buffalo Springfield Again*
18. 'Expecting To Fly' (Neil Young) – from the mono mix of *Buffalo Springfield Again*
19. 'Hung Upside Down' (Stephen Stills) – previously unreleased demo
20. 'A Child's Claim To Fame' (Richie Furay) – from the mono mix of *Buffalo Springfield Again*
21. 'Rock & Roll Woman' (Stephen Stills) – from the mono mix of *Buffalo Springfield Again*

Disc 3

Disc three is a continuation. Along with seven remastered tracks from the third and final Buffalo Springfield album *Last Time Around,* it features the last four remastered tracks from *Buffalo Springfield Again,* a full band number, a Neil Young studio jam with Buddy Miles, four demos from Neil and one demo from Richie.

'One More Sign' is a bit different. Neil's wistful, wavering voice strives for the heights on this acoustic, melodic love song. He wants to be honest, an open book, and needs to sign from his lover to confirm that everything is alright.

'The Rent Is Always Due' is another acoustic demo. This is another run-out for the song that Neil recorded for the Elektra audition. This version is much slower and less urgent, which I think suits it better. The song has matured since that first outing. The strumming pattern is totally different and the vocal is more relaxed and assured.

'Round And Round And Round' gets an early airing. A fascinating solo acoustic version of the song that finally appeared with Crazy Horse on *Everybody Knows This Is Nowhere*. Here, it has a faster strum pattern for this melancholy refrain than on that album. A very masterful, relaxed performance. It would have been fascinating to hear what Buffalo Springfield would have done with this melodic piece. I can just imagine the intermeshing guitars and soaring harmonies. There is also another version of this song with Crazy Horse on Neil's *Archives* album.

'Old Laughing Lady' is an acoustic demo of a song first offered to Buffalo Springfield that was destined to be fully produced as a track on his debut album. Here, the old laughing lady of death is given an acoustic outing. In many ways, this simple version, with its changes in tempo, is more compelling than the more developed version that appears on Neil's debut. This is a haunting vocal that captures the bleakness of the song. Simple and effective. Again, we are left wondering how Buffalo Springfield might have gone on to develop this. It would certainly have been different to the version on his first solo album.

'On The Way Home' is a slightly faster, different mix of the Neil Young song – a nice, flowing version, with Richie Furay providing the vocals to create a very listenable, melodic, commercial production. It could easily have been a single due to its pop sensibility.

'Whatever Happened To Saturday Night?' is another Neil Young song, but this is sung by Richie. This was recorded as a demo intended for the *Stampede* album that never happened. They are all there, apart from Stephen Stills. Neil is the one tapping out the piano and also adding guitar and a bit of organ, too. Richie always gives these Neil Young songs a pleasant feel and this is no exception. The band felt that Neil's voice, while distinctive, lacked a commercial edge and so sometimes got Richie on vocal duty. Together, they create a bouncy, upbeat number that seems quite at odds with the subject matter. The lyrics are about seeing his girl out with another guy – betrayal and devastation. It feels rather lightweight to me, but it would have been really interesting to hear what the full Buffalos would have done to this one, too.

Neil was into his experimental phase by the sounds of 'Falcon Lake (Ash On The Floor)'. The result was an interesting project: an instrumental medley of melodies taken from a range of Neil's own songs. You can detect 'Down By The River', 'Here We Are In The Years', 'Everybody's Alone', 'There Goes My Babe', 'Birds' and 'One More Sign'. The track features Neil playing every instrument – guitar, harmonica and piano – apart from the drums, which are provided by Buddy Miles. It sounds to me as if they were having fun in the studio and not intending to create a track to release. It flows along through its many phases. My only criticism is that it feels too light.

Tracklisting:
1. 'Hung Upside Down' (Stephen Stills) – from the mono mix of *Buffalo Springfield Again*
2. 'Good Time Boy' (Richie Furay) – from the mono mix of *Buffalo Springfield Again*
3. 'One More Sign' (Neil Young) – previously unreleased demo
4. 'The Rent Is Always Due' (Neil Young) – previously unreleased demo
5. 'Round And Round And Round' (Neil Young) – previously unreleased demo
6. 'Old Laughing Lady' (Neil Young) – previously unreleased demo
7. 'Broken Arrow' (Neil Young) – from the mono mix of *Buffalo Springfield Again*
8. 'Sad Memory' (Richie Furay) – from the mono mix of the *Buffalo Springfield Again*
9. 'On The Way Home' (Neil Young) – previously unreleased mix
10. 'Whatever Happened To Saturday Night?' (Neil Young) – previously unreleased
11. 'Special Care' (Stephen Stills) – from *Last Time Around*
12. 'Falcon Lake (Ash On The Floor)' (Neil Young) – previously unreleased
13. 'What A Day' (Richie Furay) – previously unreleased
14. 'I Am A Child' (Neil Young) – from *Last Time Around*
15. 'Questions' (Stephen Stills) – from *Last Time Around*
16. 'Merry-Go-Round' (Richie Furay) – from *Last Time Around*
17. 'Uno Mundo' (Stephen Stills) – from *Last Time Around*
18. 'Kind Woman' (Richie Furay) – from *Last Time Around*
19. 'It's So Hard To Wait' (Richie Furay & Neil Young) – from *Last Time Around*
20. 'Four Days Gone' (Stephen Stills) – previously unreleased demo

Disc 4
This is where things go a little frustratingly awry.

On the face of it, Disc 4 is great. We have a mono version of *Buffalo Springfield* and a stereo version of *Buffalo Springfield Again*. That would be great if we had not already had these tracks served up, in chronological order of their recording dates, on discs 1-3. Why repeat them? This is particularly galling when there are tracks missing from the third album and no room for the nine-minute version of 'Bluebird'. It could have been complete. It could have included Neil Young's 'Down To The Wire', which eventually came out on Neil's *Decade* collection. Then, there's the song 'Sell Out' on Neil's *Archives 1*.

Tracks 1 to 13 are the remixed mono version of their debut album. Tracks 14 to 23 are the stereo mix of their second album *Buffalo Springfield Again*.

It is great to listen to the two albums, but the frustration lies in the thought of what it might have been with those missing tracks.

All told, this is an excellent box set with some outstanding previously unheard gems and tracks of historic interest. Apart from the niggles regarding the duplication of so many tracks, the omissions of others and the missed opportunity to make it complete, it still does the job. What a band!

What's That Sound? Complete Albums Collection (2018)

This box set does exactly what it says on the cover. For those who like the flow and carefully constructed order of the original albums, and like listening to tracks in both mono and stereo, this provides exactly what you require. The first two albums are included as both mono and stereo versions, whilst only the stereo version for *Last Time Around* is included as, by this time, the recording process had made the mono recording superfluous. There were no bonus tracks. All the tracks were remastered by Neil Young and taken from the analogue master copies.

Solo Albums

Following the demise of Buffalo Springfield, Neil had the platform to do what he had always wanted to do – to produce his own albums just the way that he wanted them to be. Following the huge commercial success and critical acclaim of Buffalo Springfield, with the acknowledgement of Neil's prowess as a songwriter and musician, Neil found himself in demand. He had studio time, recording contracts and, above all, the licence to experiment and give full rein to his creativity. This was not his first foray into solo work. Previous to his spell in The Mynah Birds, he had tried his hand at going solo and that had failed miserably. While in Buffalo Springfield, he had left a few times to begin his solo career, only to go back into the fold, taking his solo efforts back with him. This time, it was for real. He had some kudos, backing and financing.

Neil's manager, Elliot Roberts, had connections. He also managed Neil's Canadian friend, and extraordinary singer/songwriter, Joni Mitchell and used his contacts with Reprise Records to get Neil a deal for a solo album. The first album, released in January 1969, was just called Neil Young. It failed to live up to commercial expectations.

Undeterred, for the second solo venture, *Everybody Knows This Is Nowhere*, released just a few months later in May 1969, Neil, in search of a more consistent sound and a rockier style, as well as a band who could support him on the road, had courted three members of The Rockets to form his backing group. They called themselves Crazy Horse. This album proved much more successful.

By the time the third solo album, *After The Gold Rush*, was released in 1970, making the Top Ten in both the UK and US, Neil was fully up and running as a highly successful solo artist. That was fully cemented with his massive fourth solo album *Harvest* in 1972, which went to number one in both countries, sold hugely and also took him to the top of the singles charts with 'Heart Of Gold'.

Running parallel to this solo career, he also found time to record and tour as a full member of the enormously successful Crosby, Stills, Nash & Young. 'I just don't like to stay in one place very long. I move around. I keep doing different things', said Neil to *Rolling Stone*.

The joy of being successful with Buffalo Springfield had given him confidence but also given him time, access to the very best musicians and facilities, removed the burden of having to make a living and allowed him to experiment and develop. Without all that, it is unlikely that he would have had the backing to get his solo career off the ground. Being hugely talented is not enough on its own.

In the course of his incredibly long solo career, he has delved into folk, country, rock 'n' roll, punk, electronic sounds, R&B, grunge and heavy metal. Whatever took his fancy. Even more incredibly, they nearly all worked.

Neil Young (1969)

Personnel:
Neil Young: vocals, guitars, piano, synthesiser, harpsichord, pipe organ
Ry Cooder: guitar, production
Jack Nitzsche: electric piano, arrangements, production
Jim Messina: bass
Carol Kaye: bass
George Grantham: drums
Earl Palmer: drums
Merry Clayton, Brenda Holloway, Patrice Holloway, Gloria Richetta Jones, Sherlie Matthews, Gracia Nitzsche: backing vocals
Unidentified: trumpet, trombone, tenor saxophone, French horn, clarinet, timpani, strings
Engineers: Dale Batchelor, Donn Landee, Mark Richardson, Henry Saskowski, Rik Pekkonen
Producers: Neil Young, David Briggs, Jack Nitzsche, Ry Cooder
Danny Kelly: photography
Ed Thrasher: album art direction
Roland Diehl: cover painting
Recorded at Wally Heider's Studio 3, Hollywood, Sunset Sound, Hollywood, TTG Los Angeles and Sunwest, Los Angeles
Label: Reprise Records
Chart positions: US: did not chart, UK: did not chart

Elliot Roberts was the manager of Buffalo Springfield (at least until Neil had him sacked). He also managed Joni Mitchell. Neil (despite having just had him sacked) asked him to manage his solo career and, incredibly, he said yes. He became pivotal in organising the deal with Reprise Records and a great recording team that put Neil's solo career into motion. It's a strange tale, as related in Neil's autobiography *Waging Heavy Peace*:

> I was sick in the hotel room with the flu and wanted something. Elliot was gone, playing golf with somebody. I decided at that moment he was never going to work as our manager and insisted we fired him. I was a spoiled brat! But what did I know? So, we fired him. The next week, I quit the Springfields for good.
>
> A few days later, I called Elliot and asked him to manage me. Was I making sense or what? That is the weirdest sequence of events I can imagine.

This solo project had been on Neil's mind for some time. He'd left Buffalo Springfield a few times in order to get stuck into the venture. At one point, he'd even recorded a song that he'd ended up putting out on Last Time Around. Now, he had the songs ready, a label and a great producer or two. Being able to work with the likes of Jack Nitzsche and Ry Cooder was a dream, although Ry treated him a little disdainfully, which did not help his fragile confidence. His reputation enabled him to attract quality musicians and the Reprise label provided the studio time. All was set.

That's where it went a bit off-kilter. To start with, they produced the album using Haeco-CSG processing, which was supposed to make the stereo album compatible with mono record players. It had the unfortunate result of lowering the quality. Added to this problem was the way the album had been mixed and produced. At this time, probably due to the way he had been treated while in Buffalo Springfield – where band members, managers and producers had been dubious about him taking the vocals because they were suspicious of his distinctive voice – Neil had developed a negative view of the timbre of his own vocal abilities. Consequently, he had put his vocals back in the mix, as explained in *Waging Heavy Peace*:

> The first mix was awful. I was trying to bury my voice because I didn't like the way it sounded... In those days, I didn't sing live, I overdubbed. I was very unsure about my singing, especially after my experiences in the studio with Green and Stone producing Buffalo Springfield.

The album was partially remixed, bringing his voice out more, and the Haeco-CSG processing was removed, just nine months later for a repress. Neil was happier, but many people preferred the earlier mix, even though one would be forgiven for thinking it was recorded through layers of cotton wool.

On this debut album, it sounds to me as if Neil is trying too hard. It is a little over-arranged and over-complicated. Everything is extremely polished. It's like a kid in a candy factory, Neil being let loose in the studio with unlimited time and lots of things to play with. I still love it, though. It demonstrates both Neil's versatility and innovation. The range of influences, from rock and country to folk, is extraordinary. There are even some heavy sounds in there. Dylan's influence is very pronounced in some areas, particularly in some of the lyrics, but it is also extremely individualistic. David Briggs claimed that it was 'a masterpiece of tones'.

The album did not sell well or generate the critical acclaim it deserved. As a debut album from a singer-songwriter, it is masterly and deserved far better appreciation. It certainly pointed to the potential that was there, even though it remains a one-off for Neil. He never recorded anything quite like it again – but then you could say that about a number of his albums. Many of them were one-offs in terms of style and content.

The lack of acclaim may be due to the centrepiece of the album, the nine-minute 'Last Trip To Tulsa' being hard to both understand or listen to. It requires concentration and serious attention, and that rather overshadows the more immediately accessible tracks, such as 'The Loner'.

When the album first came out, I was initially attracted to the cover. The artwork, based on the portrait of Neil by Roland Diehl – with surreal sky, hills

Above: Heady days with Buffalo Springfield. Neil, pictured here in 1967, displays his counter-culture credentials, with a big hat, Native American symbols, hair and sideburns. (*Henry Diltz*)

Above: The Squires circa 1963 – Ken Koblun on bass, Alan Bates on second guitar, Ken Smyth on drums and Neil Young on lead guitar and vocals.
Below: The Squires circa 1963 – a publicity shot showing Neil with Ken Koblun and Ken Smyth. The band mainly played instrumentals because they thought Neil's voice sounded odd. (*Don Baxter*)

Right: Neil playing with The Mynah Birds – a multiracial R&B band featuring Ricky Mathews (later to mutate into the funk singer Rick James), along with Neil and Bruce Palmer – circa 1965.

Left: The Mynah Birds were Canada's answer to The Rolling Stones and signed to Motown.

Right: 'It's My Time' is the Stones-sounding single released on Motown before Ricky Mathews was busted for desertion from the navy, which consequently broke up the band. (*Motown*)

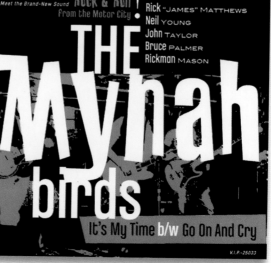

Meet the Brand-New Sound **Rock & Roll** from the Motor City

Rick "JAMES" MATTHEWS
Neil YOUNG
John TAYLOR
Bruce PALMER
Rickman MASON

THE **Mynah birds**

It's My Time b/w Go On And Cry

V.I.P.-25033

Left: The 1966 cover of Buffalo Springfield's self-titled, debut album, with a design resembling a reel of film. (*ATCO Records*)

Right: The 1967 second album *Buffalo Springfield Again* **features** a more surreal cover befitting the psychedelia of the time. (*ATCO Records*)

Left: The third and final Buffalo Springfield album, *Last Time Around,* **was** cobbled together from outtakes as the band were falling apart, with Neil leaving and coming back a number of times. (*ATCO Records*)

Right: The *Retrospective* album cover was put together by ATCO in 1969 after the band had fallen apart. (*ATCO Records*)

Left: *Buffalo Springfield* is a double album 'best of' compilation put out in 1973. (*ATCO Records*)

Right: The *Buffalo Springfield* four-CD box set, put out in 2001, is pretty comprehensive, with mono and stereo versions of the albums, all the tracks and plenty of outtakes. (*ATCO Records*)

Left: A photo of Buffalo Springfield in 1967, with Neil in the big white hat – second from the left – and Stephen Stills on the far right. (*Alamy*)

Right: An early promo shot of Buffalo Springfield in 1966 posing on the Hollywood Boulevard when everything was sweet. (*Alamy*)

Left: *What's That Sound?* is a four-CD remastered set of the three albums, with the first two albums present in both stereo and mono, but *Last Time Round* only in stereo. (*ATCO Records*)

Above: Neil, on the left, and Stephen Stills before the breakup of Buffalo Springfield, 1967. (*Alamy*)

Below: Neil in LA relaxing on a couch, 1967. (*Michael Ochs Archives*)

Left: The psychedelic cover of Neil's first solo album *Neil Young*, released in 1968. (*Reprise*)

Right: The rockier second solo album *Everybody Knows This Is Nowhere* from 1969 features the raw band Crazy Horse. (*Reprise*)

Right: The third solo album, *After The Gold Rush*, features a mixture of country folk songs interspersed with rockier numbers. (*Reprise*)

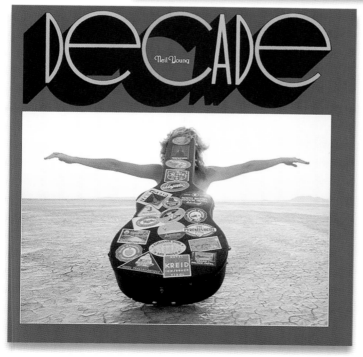

Left: *Decade* is a revolutionary 1977 triple album compilation, largely featuring old songs with a sprinkling of unreleased material. The first four sides contain material from 1966-1970. (*Reprise*)

Left: *Sugar Mountain – Live At Canterbury House* is an acoustic live show culled from three performances at the Canterbury House in Michigan in November 1968. (*Reprise*)

Right: *Live At The Riverboat 1969* is a live acoustic show from 1969 recorded at the Riverboat Coffee Bar in Toronto. (*Reprise*)

Left: *Live At The Fillmore East* is a live show from 1970 at the Fillmore East, featuring the raw energy of Crazy Horse with Danny Whitten. (*Reprise*)

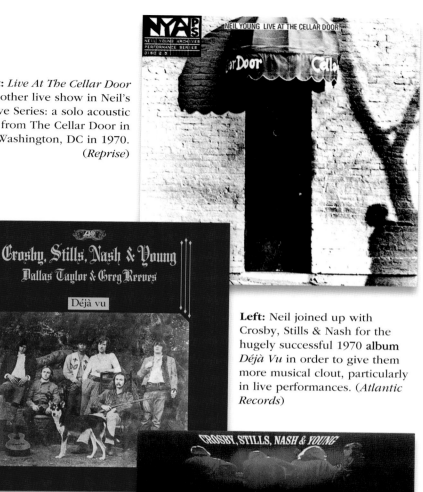

Right: *Live At The Cellar Door* is another live show in Neil's Archive Series: a solo acoustic set from The Cellar Door in Washington, DC in 1970. (*Reprise*)

Left: Neil joined up with Crosby, Stills & Nash for the hugely successful 1970 **album** *Déjà Vu* in order to give them more musical clout, particularly in live performances. (*Atlantic Records*)

Right: *Four-Way Street* is a double live album culled from performances in June and July 1970, on a tour renowned for its vicious cocaine-fuelled in-fighting as the band fell apart. (*Atlantic Records*)

Crosby, Stills, Nash & Young combine for an acoustic performance, resplendent with those spectacular close harmonies. (*CMA-Creative Management Associates/ Atlantic Records*)

Right: Neil – in the foreground – wearing his renowned leather rawhide jacket on TV, with Stephen Stills in the background. (*Michael Ochs Archives*)

Above: Graham Nash, David Crosby and Neil combine to produce some scintillating harmonies. (*Robert Altman*)

Below: Neil gazing pensively off-stage as he performs. (*Henry Diltz*)

Above: Crosby, Stills, Nash & Young in a happy, relaxed mood. (*Alamy*)

Below: Acoustic Neil in full flow. (*Chris Walter*)

Above: Fully concentrated, lost in performance. (*Larry Holst*)

Left: *Journey Through The Past* is a 1973 soundtrack album featuring some early tracks from Buffalo Springfield, live recordings and outtakes. (*Reprise*)

Right: *Carnegie Hall 1970* is a recording of Neil's first of two shows at New York's Carnegie Hall on 4 December, 1970, featuring emotive, stripped-down versions of songs to a rapt audience. (*Shakey Pictures Records*)

Left: *Neil Young Archives Vol. 1* is an impressive eight-CD box set that catalogues Neil's career for the first decade, starting with The Squires and going on to the 1970s. (*Warner Brothers*)

and reflections of a city in the water – is very colourful and striking. Being colourblind, I like garish. For me, the cover set a tone for what was inside – a vivid, surreal journey.

I already had an appreciation of Neil stemming from his work with the Buffalo Springfield and was eager to hear his solo work. My immediate reaction was that it was patchy and a shade disappointing, but as time wore on, I began discovering new depths and it proved to be an album that I played a lot. There are a number of sophisticated, quirky numbers that require multiple listens. It was not an album I found instantly accessible.

'The Emperor Of Wyoming' (Neil Young)

Neil didn't have to try to hide his vocal behind this one; maybe strangely, for a singer-songwriter, his opening solo track is an instrumental.

The country feel pervades the piece, the melody generating a Western mood with a backdrop of wide-open spaces and majestic mountains. The great drums form a platform for Neil's acoustic and electric guitar, augmented with orchestration. There is nothing complex about the archetypal melody line, with its comfortable ambling beat.

David Briggs produced this and is widely thought to be the inspiration for the track, as he originally comes from Wyoming, although Stephen Stills is another contender.

Neil's guitar work is distinctive, with characteristic riffs and trademark triplets. Briggs said that Neil's vibrato lead guitar, delivering the soaring notes of the melody, was created by putting the guitar through a Leslie speaker to create 'psycho guitar noises'.

'The Loner' (Neil Young)

There is a complete change of style for this number. We jump into a much heavier sound. The rhythm section is tremendous (Jim Messina on bass, George Grantham on drums). They set up a real tough, driving sound. At times, that chugging bass really churns. The number is propelled along by that superb heavy riff, but it evolves through a gentle middle eight. Such energy. The blending of guitar, in double drop D tuning, with attenuated squeals, is sublime. Neil's vocal is drenched in pathos.

Many see this song as an autobiographical take on Neil's life, and particularly his difficulty in fitting into a band like Buffalo Springfield; others see it as being about Stephen Stills. Neil is keeping quiet on the matter. Having said that, the second verse is kind of sinister, giving a view of a voyeuristic stalker, which puts a different twist on the concept of this loner.

The immediate impression of the lyric is that it is an expression of Neil's own withdrawn character. Maybe it isn't meant to be autobiographical at all and the character is a more deviant kind of person possessing much more menace. Suddenly, Neil's loner appears to be more threatening.

For reasons I cannot comprehend, when released as a single, it failed to chart. There is no justice. For me, it is the outstanding track on the album and I guess Neil likes it too because it's been a stalwart in his stage act ever since! That riff is chilling!

'If I Could Have Her Tonight' (Neil Young)
There is yet another change of style for this Jack Nitzsche production. This is more like the Buffalo Springfield sound. The drum and bass are to the fore, but it is based around acoustic guitars, with some steel guitar thrown in for good measure. The beautiful wafting electric guitar notes towards the end are Ry Cooder.

This is an openly romantic song, full of honesty and longing. Neil's gentle vocal perfectly captures the sense of craving. It's a girl that he's missing. It wasn't the right time when they met; now he's wondering what it would be like. He's sounding very vulnerable and needful.

'I've Been Waiting For You' (Neil Young)
You can feel the desperation bubbling up in this Neil Young classic. It has everything. The Neil Young signature is all over it. The descending guitar riff sucks you in with its heavy chords creating a compulsive hook – a real killer. The rhythm section is forceful, setting the pace towards a vertiginous crescendo. The guitar solo is one of Neil's best, full of menace. Then, we have the tinkling keyboards sitting a little back in the mix.

You need earphones in order to get the full flavour of the complex arrangement.

Neil's voice is full of that yearning that amply suits the lyrics. He's been waiting for this magic woman for a long time.

'The Old Laughing Lady' (Neil Young)
This is another Jack Nitzsche production. You can hear that instantly through the arrangement of those strings. Ry Cooder is in there somewhere, too.

Neil is supposed to have written this on a napkin in a coffee house and claims not to know what the inspiration was. The focus seems quite clear to me, though – the major theme appears to be death. That old laughing lady comes for you in many guises: a slip on the stairs, too much booze, on the freeway, in your bed. But then Neil's lyrics often read like Zen poetry. The ambiguity is intriguing. He first recorded it as a demo back in the days of Buffalo Springfield.

The music is just as beguiling, with its changes of tempo and varying sections. Neil said that the double drop D tuning gives it depth and grandeur that adds to its sweet sadness. Jack Nitzsche applied a pre-echo technique that muted the vocals. The effect is complex and absorbing. The textured drums are provided by Earl Palmer. The bass, which starts as a slow, steady pulsing heartbeat, is played by Jim Messina. The acoustic guitars set up some great rhythms while the strings waft in and out, perfectly synchronised, and a piano adds sprinkles of notes over the countermelodies.

The music changes towards the end, as a female-sung chorus breaks in with an eerie quality – the spooky sound of death – and the song grooves its way to the end, as a lone piano sees us out to the finish.

'String Quartet From Whiskey Boot Hill' (Neil Young)

Just as the first side starts with an instrumental, so does the second. Although the title suggests another country Western theme, the music doesn't do that for me. It says it's from Whiskey Boot Hill, but I can't see the connection.

As the name suggests, this is a delicate, beautiful string quartet composition lasting for one minute. It leads, with piano notes, straight into the next track 'Here We Are In The Years'.

Neil was working on this composition back in 1967. It was later incorporated (along with 'Down Down Down' and 'Country Girl I Think You're Pretty') into the track 'Country Girl' on the Crosby, Still, Nash and Young album *Déjà Vu*.

'Here We Are In The Years' (Neil Young)

Back in those halcyon days of the sixties, so brimming with optimism, there was a general feeling that modern life had gone wrong. With all the pollution, aggression, war and boredom of mainstream existence, we'd lost something about the joy of connecting to nature. A number of sixties kids looked at their parents' lives, with their boring jobs and suburban empty lifestyle, and saw them as dreary. They rebelled against it.

Lives become careers.
Children cry in fear.
Let us out of here!

There was a move among the hippie culture to end that dislocation, to return to the country and enjoy a simpler life. Instead of ridiculing farmers and their slower pace, there was a desire to get back to the land, to adopt a slower, quieter, more peaceful and less destructive lifestyle with more meaning, closer to nature. This song taps straight into that concept.

While people planning trips to stars
Allow another boulevard to claim
A quiet country lane
It's insane.

The song is only a short three minutes but has many sections with changes in tempo, instrumentation and mood. It begins with a solitary piano before the rhythm section enters, followed by guitars. Overall, this is a soft, lilting song that is both mellow and laid-back.

The song builds with added instrumentation – a horn, strings – as the melody flows through different sections. Neil's vocal is in his higher register, expressive and aching with pain. Very beautiful, but packed with emotion.

'What Did You Do To My Life?' (Neil Young)
You have to admire Neil's honesty. Nothing is off the table. All life's experiences are grist to the mill. This song focuses on the break-up of a long-term relationship, leaving him bereft.

It isn't fair that I should wake up at dawn and not find you there
(What did you do to my life?)
I don't care if all of the mountains turn to dust in the air
(What did you do to my life?)

That fuzzy lead guitar through the Leslie speaker is a little at odds with the acoustic strumming and gentle rhythm section. Neil's pained voice creates a memorable song out of a pitiful experience. The chorus is particularly melodic, and the distant wailing chorus coming in from far away carries the emotional impact. She's left him and his life is wrecked. Ah, the intensity of love.

'I've Loved Her So Long' (Neil Young)
A track that is based upon a wonderfully bright, busy, intricate bass line with slow drums and a generous dressing of luscious strings. Not a guitar in sight (or sound). Neil is looking at this gorgeous girl from afar as she makes a mess of her life. Only Neil can save this errant young lady from herself as she 'tumbles by and rolls along, getting it all wrong'. He could sort things out and bring her peace.

As on the entire album, Neil's voice is in the higher register, delicate and full of emotion. It suits this type of gentle rendition and blends well with the strings. The female chorus and backing add a level of anguish that enhances the overt craving in Neil's voice.

'The Last Trip To Tulsa' (Neil Young)
The most Dylan-esque of Neil's songs, and yet not Dylan at all. This apparently surreal dream sequence of dissociated images, tumbling out in a stream of consciousness, is truly bizarre. It sounds as strange to me now as it did back in 1968 when I first lowered it onto my turntable. Looking for meaning or a thread through this strange fantasy landscape is like trying to find rational logic in a Dali painting. It's nine and a half minutes of images to wonder at. I used to just put it on and allow it to flow through my ears and tease my imagination. Sometimes, snippets seem to make perfect sense, but I can't imagine Neil as a taxi driver or woman. A folk singer, yes! He'd done that unsuccessfully in Toronto back in 1965: 'I used to be a folk singer, keeping managers alive. When you saw me on a corner and told me I was jive'.

The fact that the arrangement is just Neil strumming an acoustic guitar only serves to make the Dylan comparison more real, though Neil's high, smooth, strained voice couldn't be more unlike Dylan, and the lyrics are even more surreal than anything Dylan ever did.

As for the content, well, I've read all manner of explanations, ranging from acid trips, visions of the end of the world, reliving of past lives and reincarnation, but the truth is more mundane: Neil was riding in a car to Tulsa, reading articles in a newspaper and stringing them together to create the song. Here's what seems to me to be a good explanation for some of the lines straight from Neil: 'I heard a siren scream. Pulled over to the corner and I fell into a dream. There were two men eating pennies and three young girls who cried'. The two guys were pulled over by the cops and were eating their joints (one-tenth of a dime bag – pennies) so they wouldn't be busted. They were wanted for raping three young girls.

The next article was about an earthquake in California: 'The West Coast is falling; I see rocks in the sky. The preacher took his bible and laid it on the stool'. Then a dead woman woke up on the autopsy table: 'Well, I used to be asleep, you know, with blankets on my bed. I stayed there for a while till they discovered I was dead. The coroner was friendly, I liked him quite a lot'. Then, an article about the Vietnam War, where they put green dye in the military petrol to identify it because it was being stolen by the Vietnamese: 'Well, I was driving down the freeway when my car ran out of gas. Pulled over to the station, but I was afraid to ask. The servicemen were yellow and the gasoline was green. Although I knew I couldn't, I thought that I was gonna scream'. The last section was about an 87-year-old man who was killed by a palm tree which fell on him while he was chopping it down: 'No, it's not a case of being lonely we have here. I've been working on this palm tree for 87 years'.

You see, nothing here is surreal or acid-based at all. Not even a dream. It is merely an artistic juxtapositioning of different stories from a newspaper, provided with a big dollop of Neil's creative imagination and magic fairy dust. If Neil hadn't explained it, who would ever have worked that out for themselves?

Related Tracks:
'Sugar Mountain' (Neil Young)
'Sugar Mountain' was one of Neil's early tracks – a staple of his early solo performances and, at the time, only available as the B-side on the rare 'The Loner' single (it was strangely released as the B-side of two later singles and only received an official album release in 1977 on *Decade*). Incredibly, given the quality of the track, the single failed to chart anywhere.

The previous recording of this song was on the audition tape for Elektra Records in 1965. The song had musically developed since then, becoming more sophisticated with an intricate strum pattern providing a stronger melody. Lyrically, it remained unchanged since the time Neil wrote it. He claims to have written the lyrics out while under the stairs in a flophouse in Ontario after leaving the Squires and at the time of meeting up with Stephen Stills. The song is one of desperation – the realisation that he was leaving something precious behind. He was becoming old. Fifty-odd years on, I can still remember that feeling. There was a sense that it was all over. At 21, you were past it.

It was a very important song in that it showed a progression into a different level of songwriting (inspired by Dylan and Ochs) involving a greater poetic depth. He sang it in his brief, unsuccessful solo folk period, during which he met Joni Mitchell. She was a little alarmed by this fatalistic attitude and wrote 'Circle Song' to put more of a positive spin on Neil's jaundiced view.

Neil claims to have written 126 verses to this song. Maybe someday, we'll get to hear a few more of those verses. Neil has always been a great one for not discarding anything and eventually recycling it all. Just imagine, a whole album of 'Sugar Mountain' in all its 126 verse majesty!

Everybody Knows This Is Nowhere (With Crazy Horse) (1969)

Personnel:
Neil Young: guitar, lead vocals
Danny Whitten: guitar, harmony vocals, co-lead vocal on 'Cinnamon Girl'
Billy Talbot: bass guitar
Ralph Molina: drums, harmony vocals
Bobby Notkoff: violin on 'Running Dry (Requiem For The Rockets)'
Robin Lane: harmony vocal on 'Round And Round'
Producers: Neil Young, David Briggs
Engineers: David Briggs, Henry Saskowski, Kendal Pacios
Recorded at Wally Heider's Studio 3, Hollywood
Label: Reprise
Chart position: US: 34

Neil has never been short of creative energy. Having poured his dynamism into the first solo album, he was by no means spent. As soon as that was out of the way, Neil was thinking of what to do next. Jimmy McDonough, in *Shakey,* related how he found himself captivated by the idea of putting his own band together and producing a far rockier sound: 'I wanna cross Dylan and The Stones'. All the acoustic, country and folk styles were abandoned, along with those luscious strings and delicate arrangements. This was going to be very different. In many respects, this was a monumental album, a change of style to gritty garage rock, a low-tech approach with that loose, grungey infusion of blues and fabulous sloppy guitar breaks that were to become a regular of Neil's future act and give him credibility as a leading rock guitarist. Neil rips the guts out of his guitar to create a collage of sound, blistering blasts of angry noise and riffs that were sonic explosions. All the finesse and complexity of Buffalo Springfield and the first album was shelved. This was raw power: Neil told *Rolling Stone* that 'Crazy Horse is funkier, simpler, more down to the roots'.

Neil was refinding that primaeval force that had turned him on to rock music as a kid: 'Rock 'n' roll is fire, man, FIRE. It's thumbing your nose against the world', David Briggs said. Neil agreed. This was not about sophistication; this was about feel and energy.

Neil had been taken with an L.A. band called The Rockets, whom he had jammed with a number of times. He approached them with a view to working together. Danny Whitten, Billy Talbot and Ralph Molina were brought into the fold. Their rough energy was just what Neil was looking for. They looked for a name that might suit their maverick primaeval style and, with Neil being a big admirer of the Native American Indian way of life, selected the name Crazy Horse. Crazy Horse was a much-celebrated Chief of the Sioux tribe. He took his name from his father and a vision he had seen of him riding a prancing horse, painted in a specific way. While he and the horse were painted in such a manner, they could not be harmed. He fearlessly led his warriors into battle on his painted prancing horse. The vision of this wild, proud Sioux Chief seemed to sum up the raw vitality and renegade spirit of the band.

Just four months after that polished first album, Neil and his new band were back in the studio working on a new, totally different type of album. Incredibly, it seems that the backbone of the album, four incredibly important tracks – 'Cinnamon Girl', 'Cowgirl In the Sand', 'Everybody Knows This Is Nowhere' and 'Down By The River' were all written in one single day. Neil had been ill with a temperature of 103 °F (39.5 °C): 'Sometimes, if you get sick, get a fever, it's easy to write. Everything opens up', Neil said to Jimmy McDonough in *Shakey*. His overheated brain had obviously greatly stimulated some creative centre in his cerebral cortex. What incredible songs they were. Not a dud between them. Songs that were destined to be part of his stage act right up to the present time.

Having a band allowed Neil to extend his songs with long, improvised instrumental passages. Two of the tracks are very long: one over ten minutes and one over nine minutes. This meant that he only needed seven tracks in order to complete the album. Crazy Horse were primitive and raw, going for power and feel rather than complexity. They provided Neil with a blank canvas of pulsing rhythm for him to paint on, to unleash his vocals and let his Les Paul, Old Black, freak out. They provided the base on which the unfettered Young, like Lichtenstein, was liberated to drip, throw and spray his colours. The result is like comparing the great daubs of bright colour of Van Gogh with the delicate, intricate brushwork of Vermeer. There's no comparison. It wasn't about musicianship. It was all about that primordial force. It was the chemistry of the band that was important to Neil. They were not the greatest of musicians, but they seemed to have an intuitive feel that enabled Neil to relax and flow with it. They zoned out together. In particular, Danny Whitten seemed to bring out the best in Neil. The way their guitars and vocals sparred was spontaneously electric. In *Shakey*, Jimmy McDonough asked Neil about the importance of Danny Whitten: 'What did Danny bring to Crazy Horse? The glue. The glue that held it all together'.

What Neil was proving was that, although, to my ears, he did not possess a 'good' voice, in terms of its tonal quality, he did possess an interesting voice capable of both great intensity and expressiveness. On this album, his voice is lower and more powerful and he shows that he could manage the full range. That versatility would be put to good use throughout the length of his career, as he moved through different genres of music. He was able to lose that complex about his voice for good – and it showed. In *Shakey*, he told Jimmy McDonough: 'That's when a change came over me. Right then'.

Everybody Knows This Is Nowhere is a rock album that redefined Neil's career. In *Shakey*, Neil is quoted as saying: 'I knew that it was a good record.

I also knew it was raw. I knew that it was us'. It propelled him into a different hemisphere. He was no longer the singer-songwriter languishing in the shadow of Dylan; he was a fully-fledged rock star. The album also reversed his poor commercial showing. It reached a respectable number 34 on the album charts and went gold the following year. It has since gone platinum.

'Cinnamon Girl' (Neil Young)
When I first heard that incredible riff, it blew my mind. I hadn't heard anything quite as dynamite as that for a long time – and it's still one of the greatest heavy riffs in rock music – right up there with 'You Really Got Me', 'Brown Sugar', 'Whole Lotta Rosie' and 'Big Eyed Beans From Venus', not that Neil is comparable with any of those. The powerful interaction between those two guitars is incredibly effective. The basic riff is primitive and visceral. The way the two guitars interact only serves to enhance that rawness so that it hits you right in the belly. Neil is playing his Les Paul Gibson 'Old Black' in a funky double D (DADGBD) tuning to create those thunderous power chords, that have since been called proto-grunge. When I bought that album, I kept putting that needle right back to this track, played it endlessly and never got tired of it. Still, 55 years later, I haven't had my fill. It's timeless.

What was so exciting was the rawness of it. Having liked the sophistication and delicate nature of the first album, with Neil's anguished vocals in that high-end – squeezed through his larynx – I now adored the full open-throat power. It felt like Neil was free. He wasn't holding back or restricted in any way. It felt like he was having fun. He'd finally come to terms with his voice, which gells so well with Danny Whitten's high-supporting vocals. It gives the track real energy.

We'd all like to spend our lives with a spicy Cinnamon Girl. In the *Decades* liner notes, Neil says: 'Wrote this for a city girl on peeling pavement coming at me thru Phil Ochs' eyes playing finger cymbals. It was hard to explain to my wife'. His wife at the time was Susan Acevedo (who may or may not have served him cinnamon pancakes in her Topanga Canyon café), but the song was at least partially about Jean Glover (who played finger cymbals with her husband, Jim Glover). They were friends of Phil Ochs and Neil had a crush on Jean. 'Cowgirl In The Sand' was also thought to be inspired by Jean.

'Everybody Knows This Is Nowhere' (Neil Young)
Another hot dose of Crazy Horse on what is a deliberate, electrified country style – Crazy Horse rock. That bass thumps right through you. Those guitars blend and burn with a good deal of distortion. The chord sequence is complex – G C Em7 A C/B Am7 Gmaj7 – though the strum rhythms are fairly basic. I never get tired of hearing how those guitars intermesh. There's real creative freedom in the way they groove together, feeding off each other. They've really rocked country up into something else by adding in a dose of Rolling Stones dirt. On top of that, Danny Whitton's high falsetto backing vocals, with all those 'La La's, are exquisite.

The song sums up Neil's current disillusionment with the Los Angeles music scene, with all its 'Day-to-day running around'. He needs to have a break: 'I'd like to go back home and take it easy'. There's no oblique poetry in the song; he's just telling it like it is. He doesn't want to be on the pop treadmill anymore; he's had enough. He wants out of the stifling heat of L.A. and is dreaming of the cool breezes of country life back in Canada. The feeling is so strong that he named the whole album after it. You can hear how much he means it. The country feel reflects the sentiment. Even though they rock, it has an easy feel to the music.

The vocal track of Neil's is actually the guide vocal he laid down for the band to follow. They decided that it was so full of conviction that they'd keep it instead of 'properly' recording the vocal through better mics with reverb. Works great for me. This is the ultimate song of the big hippie dream to escape to the countryside and be back in tune with nature.

'Round & Round (It Won't Be Long)' (Neil Young)

This is an acoustic gem of huge emotional impact – the first recording with Crazy Horse. The acoustic guitars begin the track, churning and melding. The vocals come in and delicately blend. Robin Lane's voice, with its lilt and emphasis, fits so perfectly, adding a perfect foil for Neil, and Danny Whitten provides that higher end. The music and voices create a hypnotic, circular pattern, reflecting the routine of life. You can feel they are all lost in it, mesmerised by the configuration they are creating. The circular rhythm is punctuated with fills that provide momentum and drive the track onto its repeating motif. The voices literally ooze with sadness. Neil explains the track's vocals in *Waging Heavy Peace*:

> We all sang live on 'Round And Round': Danny, Robin and me, all gathered in a circle like at Laurel Canyon, singing and playing. The vocals are so great – Danny singing at the top and Robin's rich voice on the bottom. Danny's soulful acoustic playing. Amazing. That whole album is so pure.

In a very different way, this is a track mimicking the same sentiments as on the last track 'Everybody Knows This Is Nowhere'. It's a song of disillusionment mixed with the endless metronomic passing of time and visions of mortality.

Neil is looking at life and how we all construct our own prisons, through the ruts of our habits in our day-to-day existence, instead of living: 'Round and round and round we spin to weave a wall to hem us in'. We stop ourselves from connecting with what is real. He wants off this wheel and into something more real and less damaging. And that life damages us. It's all too short to live like this. 'How slow and slow it goes to mend the tear that always shows. It won't be long, it won't be long'. And we see our friends beaten down and destroyed by the way they are living, ending in despair:

'And you see your best friend looking over the end and you turn to see why, and he looks in your eyes and he cries'. He is describing the pathetic helplessness of an addict contemplating his own demise. The irony of this line is that, all too soon, Danny Whitten would end up a victim and then Bruce Berry.

It's a song that has come in for some criticism from a number of quarters. I can only assume that they haven't connected with either the incredible emotional depth or the melodic beauty of the piece. For me, it has both in spades.

'Down By The River' (Neil Young)

This is another of those tracks that came out of Neil's fever spell – a brain-boiling temperature that unleashed a burst of creativity. On the face of it, this is a murder ballad about shooting his unfaithful girlfriend, but it isn't really. It could be a number of things. Ending a drug addiction has been mooted, but Neil has said it was really about the ending of a relationship and lost love. I guess that a feverish mind would come up with many visions, murder being one of them.

'We were playing the song and it opened up into this long jam', bassist Billy Talbot recalled to *Uncut* magazine in 2021. 'The three of us were used to doing that and Neil just stayed there with us'. The guitar starts off at a chugging pace on this nine-minute track, the second guitar coming in over the top. The drums strike up a steady pace, and when that booming bass comes in, it reaches fusion. Neil's vocal is anguished and Danny Whitten adds that higher-end backing vocal to give it energy. The chorus is so melodic that it melts into your mind. The dominant bass sets up a circular repeating motif and we come to the incredible jamming solo in which Neil lets loose with his Les Paul – Old Black. Starting with a single note stuttering and hanging, the guitar becomes more manic and strangled, shrieking its way towards the end. Crazy Horse, out of their previous experience and familiarity, provide a solid base for Neil to unleash his power and produce jamming at its very best. The track motors for nine minutes and not a single note or second is boring. The power is immense.

'The Losing End (When You're On)' (Neil Young)

Another change of texture with an unabashed country ballad. This band can rock in so many different ways. The versatility on this album is exceptional – hard rocking grunge to delicate country ballads. It's all there.

Crazy Horse create a fairly standard country backing for Neil to work his magic on. The harmonies with Danny Whitten are, once again, right up there with the best. The slow, melodic tale is an earworm that gets you whistling the tune for days. Neil's voice, at times, becoming an exaggerated country drawl a la Hank Williams, is infectious. It is a break-up song about an unfaithful woman who has up and left him. There's a pleading in the voice.

Won't she change, settle down and come back? 'Won't you ever change your ways? It's so hard to make love pay when you're on the losing end'. At the time, Neil was married to Susan Acevedo, whom he divorced a year later, but there's no indication that it was about her.

'Running Dry (Requiem For The Rockets)' (Neil Young)

Now, this is one that Neil has stated was about Susan Acevedo, but, from the title, one might assume that it is also a lament of regret for his part in breaking up The Rockets. We're heading into an electrified piece of folk music based on the old Irish traditional song from around 1870 called 'Spancil Hill'. What we end up with is by no means folk or Irish, as Neil applies his anguished rock-tinged vocals and the band provide a raw backing of repeating picked guitar patterns. Bobby Notkoff, from The Rockets, provides the most emotive violin you're ever going to hear. It adds a full punch of pathos to this lament, capturing the full spectrum of anguish and misery.

This is yet another break-up song full of penitence and sorrow. This time, he's blaming himself: 'I'm sorry for the things I've done; I've shamed myself with lies. My cruelty has punctured me and now I'm running dry'.

'Cowgirl In The Sand' (Neil Young)

For the last track on the album, we're treated to ten minutes of unrelenting hard rock straight out of Neil's fever-addled mind, with a great slab of improvisation thrown in – ten minutes of wondrous heavy riffs, brutal guitar assaults and beautifully articulated verses.

Incongruously, it starts with some gentle semi-acoustic guitar. There is a pause, like a gathering of breath, the wind dropping before the storm, and then the band kick in with their memorable and unique heavy riffs. Ralph Molina's drumming provides the energy and Billy Talbot's bass sets up powerful patterns and thundering sections. Two guitars interplay nicely, Neil's unleashing primal, brutal licks, searing notes and stinging barbs of sound. We're transported into Crazy Horse's powerful spell, in which Neil is delighting in letting fly with full fury. They intuitively feed off each other to create this storm of improvised rock. At odds with the musical interludes, the three verses are sung with a melodic control that is juxtaposed with the stridency of the instruments – yet, it all gels perfectly.

The lyrical content is purposefully ambiguous and open to interpretation. Nothing is straightforward. Is this about one woman/girl or two? About his marriage break-up with Susan Acevedo or his ongoing obsession with his first love? A relationship with a groupie or an idealized woman? Is it based on the beach in Spain or is the dust and rust the symbols of intransigence? This woman, these women, is/are strong, determined and independent. There's an accusatory vein of betrayal and lack of trust, of infidelity with wedding bands rusting, but also of pining, yearning and wishful hoping. For me, each verse seems to be about a particular woman that Neil has had an attachment to –

the young girl who liked to flirt with the boys, the married woman who was a powerful sexual partner and the idealised woman of his dreams, who, for some reason, he rejected.

Perhaps Neil needed that flu-ridden brain to provide a set of strange images and thoughts. He was relaying scenes that were playing inside his skull. Addled dreams that, while lacking in complete coherence, were, nonetheless, communicating their essence in some primitive manner. The pictures were vivid, as the high temperature of his cortex conjured up disconnected, intriguing images. All the songs he produced during that feverish period seem to have similar qualities. Very visual. Very open to interpretation, extremely ambiguous, but very strong.

Singles
'Everybody Knows This Is Nowhere' b/w 'The Emperor Of Wyoming'
The track 'Everybody Knows This Is Nowhere' has a number of versions. It was originally recorded for inclusion on Neil's debut album but was not included. That version had a very different arrangement to the Crazy Horse one, incorporating a variety of woodwind instruments and strings to create a much more sophisticated, wistful and delicate sound – lacking the fire and passion of the album version.

The single version is a slightly shorter take, gentler and mellow, recorded without Crazy Horse and, hence, lacking the strident guitars and Danny Whitten's backing vocals. There's even a little burst of what sounds like a recorder. It was released prior to the album as a taster, but why a different version was chosen is a mystery. Not too many copies were sold and it failed to chart anywhere.

This single version was eventually put out on Neil's *Archives Vol. 1* boxset.

'Down By The River' b/w 'The Losing End (When You're On)'
These two tracks were lifted straight from the album but failed to chart.

'Oh Lonesome Me' b/w 'I've Been Waiting For You'
'Oh Lonesome Me' had been recorded but not included on the album. It was later released on *After The Gold Rush*. The B-side was another strange choice, being directly lifted from the debut album. Despite being a completely new track and a very warm, accessible number, it, too, failed to dent the charts. *Rolling Stone* obviously liked it: 'Buy 'Oh Lonesome Me' and let Neil Young and Crazy Horse haunt you for four minutes'.

Conclusion
The album is over. What a feast. The experiment with Crazy Horse has led to something strong, vital and novel. What is clear is that Neil found the confines of Buffalo Springfield, with its intricate harmonies, choreographed precision and delicate intermeshing guitars, far too claustrophobic. He did not enjoy

being part of a pop group with all the trappings that entailed. His debut solo album was too cautious and controlled, but Crazy Horse released him to give full vent to his entire pent-up vocal, lyrical and instrumental instincts. You can feel the freedom. You can feel the unbridled joy. This was Neil at full gallop. Crazy Horse had unleashed him. From that moment on, there was no turning back. He'd really found his feet, his voice, his confidence, his style and his freedom.

After The Gold Rush (1970)

Personnel:
Neil Young: guitar, piano, harmonica, vibes, lead vocals
Danny Whitten: guitar, vocals
Nils Lofgren: guitar, piano, vocals
Jack Nitzsche: piano
Billy Talbot: bass
Greg Reeves: bass
Ralph Molina: drums, vocals
Stephen Stills: vocals
Bill Peterson: flugelhorn
Producers: Neil Young, David Briggs with Kendall Pacios
Recorded at Hollywood, CA Sound City, and Redwood Studios, Topanga, CA
Label: Reprise Records
Chart positions: US: 8, UK: 7

Things were happening fast. Neil's solo career had just taken off with the rockin' *Everybody Knows This Is Nowhere*; he'd left the crazy hype and demands of Buffalo Springfield in his wake and was free to do what he wanted. But life isn't like that. There are no easy, straightforward choices – just decisions and difficult choices. Indecision ruled. This should have been easy, but it wasn't.

Having found his voice with Crazy Horse, and, particularly, with Danny Whitten, Neil discovered that Danny was falling apart with his drug addictions. That made things hard.

Following the demise of Buffalo Springfield, Stephen Stills had teamed up with David Crosby and Graham Nash to create Crosby, Stills & Nash and they'd gone stratospheric with their debut album. With the desire to record a follow-up and go on tour, the band decided that they required more musical power. They called on Neil. Despite all the immense pressures of fame with Buffalo Springfield and a tempestuous relationship with Stills, Neil was tempted. He liked what he heard, liked the band members and could see a place for himself.

On top of that, Neil had bought himself a wooden cabin out in the wilderness of Topanga Canyon, to the side of Laurel Canyon out of L.A. – he had made his idealistic return to the country. 'I love nature. To me, nature is a church', he told Jimmy McDonough in *Shakey*. He was enjoying being out of the rat race of the L.A. music scene and looking forward to a more natural, laid-back lifestyle. Jimmy reported him as saying: 'I look at the planet and all I see is proof that we need to change'. Laurel Canyon and Topanga Canyon were where the bohemian community of artists and musicians hung out. Very free and easy. Topanga Canyon was also where he met up with and married Susan Acevedo, who ran the Topanga Canyon café where Neil used to drop in for breakfast. Elliot Roberts said in *Shakey* that *After The Gold Rush* was Neil's Topanga Canyon album – 'It was a soft record and much more writerly. It propelled Neil into that writer class with Leonard Cohen, James Taylor and Joni'.

What should have been an easy course of action – to go back into the studio with Crazy Horse, record a follow-up album and go on the road to promote his solo career – had suddenly become complicated. The temptation proved far too strong and Neil, instead of taking the offer to support CS&N in the studio and on tour, held out to be taken on as a full member of the band. Crosby, Stills & Nash became Crosby, Stills, Nash & Young and Neil found himself back in the spotlight with commitments to produce material, record, tour and promote. It was the start of another tempestuous set of band politics, demands and difficult relationships that was going to resound down through the decades, give rise to many fall-outs, much heat and a great deal of wonderful music. It also meant that Neil's creativity was split. Instead of it all being directed into his solo efforts, part of it had to be given to CSN&Y. After hauling himself out of the cauldron of fame and excessive demands, he had climbed right back into the frying pan of celebrity.

By the time of *After The Gold Rush*, CSN&Y had recorded and released their massive *Déjà Vu* album, which had taken the world by storm, sold millions and propelled CSN&Y to being one of the top acts in rock music. This was much bigger than even Buffalo Springfield had been. The success of CSN&Y had set the bar higher. It also provided a platform for the individual band members. They all released highly successful solo albums in the wake of *Déjà Vu*. During the course of 1970/71, Stephen Stills released *Stills*, David Crosby released *If I Could Only Remember My Name* and Graham Nash released *Songs For Beginners*.

Neil went into the studio in Hollywood with Crazy Horse to record his own new solo effort. It wasn't working. Danny Whitten wasn't together. He was strung out on heroin. The music just did not flow as easily. He already had 'Birds' in the can from an earlier session and managed to salvage two other tracks – 'I Believe In You' and 'Oh Lonesome Me'. Hardly the free-form rockin' songs from *Everybody Knows This Is Nowhere*.

In a quandary, Neil had to go off and tour with CSN&Y, having not created as much as he would have liked. When he came back, he'd made some decisions. Firstly, he decided to set up his own makeshift studio in the basement of his cabin in Topanga Canyon, which he named Redwood Studios (after the redwood panelling in his cabin). He was hoping that the more relaxed atmosphere would prove fruitful. Secondly, he decided to expand the personnel. He was aiming for a kind of amalgamation of Crazy Horse and CSN&Y. He brought his great friend, dynamite musician and rival Stephen Stills in, as well as Jack Nitzsche and CSN&Y's Greg Reeves, and made the strange, gut decision of bringing in the 18-year-old, exceptionally talented Nils Lofgren on keyboards (an instrument he was not used to) to augment Crazy Horse. A third component was that Neil had badly injured his back lifting a huge slab of wood and had to wear a back brace. That severely limited his movement and made playing the electric guitar difficult. He had to be seated. 'I was in and out of hospital for two years between *After The Gold Rush* and *Harvest*. My discs slipped'.

With all of this in mind, they set to work to craft an album of eclectic styles with elements of folk, country and rock. It was not a return to the overdubbed sophistication of the first album or a continuation of the Crazy Horse rawness of the second. This fell somewhere in between. By the end, Neil was fed up with Topanga, as well as L.A. It wasn't providing him with the peace he required. In *Shakey*, Neil comments that: 'I didn't like L.A. or Topanga. Too busy. Too many weirdos'.

I was 21 when the album came out, living in London in the midst of the alternative counter-culture underground. The dream was beginning to fade, but the psychedelic/acid rock/folk scene was still going strong. I was greatly looking forward to another slab of the improvised hard-rockin' music I had loved on *Everybody Knows This Is Nowhere*. This was different. The moods were different. There were some of those hard rock numbers, like 'Southern Man', but also delicate country numbers, like 'Lonesome Me'. It took me a while to assimilate and appreciate the range. One thing that was immediately clear to me was that no matter what style Neil was working in, he made it his own.

The title and inspiration for the album had come from a screenplay called *After The Gold Rush* by Herb Berman and Dean Stockwell. I was familiar with the elusive acid poet Herb Berman, who had worked with Captain Beefheart to produce the incredible lyrics on The Magic Band's first two albums. That seemed like a great connection to me. With its folk and country songs and tighter production, this was a move more towards the CSN&Y style.

The solarised photo on the cover, of a pensive Neil passing a little old lady walking in the opposite direction, seems to sum up the content. This is a slab of introspection.

'Tell Me Why' (Neil Young)

Instead of the incendiary opening riffs of 'Cinnamon Girl', we are presented with a melodic acoustic country/folk song. Neil is accompanied by Nils Lofgren, producing a crisp, rich-sounding strumming from two guitars tuned down to D. The melody, delivered by Neil, is lifted by the addition of Crazy Horse harmonies on the chorus. There is no other backing.

The lyrics set out as we mean to go on. Neil is still trying to come to terms with himself and what he wants to do with his life: 'Tell me why, tell me why. Is it hard to make arrangements with yourself, when you're old enough to repay but young enough to sell?' It seems that as an era is winding down, Neil, like many of his contemporaries, was struggling to understand the world and their place in it.

'After The Gold Rush' (Neil Young)

This is one of the two songs directly related to the never-produced film script of the same name. This poignant track is sparse in terms of arrangement – just Neil tinkling the piano and a very poignant flugelhorn section, played by Bill Peterson, arrives later on. Neil delivers his most moving and delicate falsetto, and it is extremely effective in this context. The melody whistles around in your head. The emotion is heartfelt.

The film script describes an apocalyptic scene of destruction, as California, the scene of the Great Gold Rush, is destroyed in a devastating flood. At the time, Neil was very keen on making it happen with himself, Dennis Hopper and Janis Joplin, but Universal Studios thought it was too much of a risk with a bunch of crazy hippies. Neil took the theme further with the help of a dream (probably marijuana enhanced), to envisage the destruction of the entire planet brought about by our own greed. He looked at the sprawl and pollution of L.A. and saw what we were doing to the planet – 'When I look out the window, the first thing that comes to my mind is the way this place looked a hundred years ago'.

He then produced three verses based on different periods of time. The first centres on the medieval period, with a pristine earth and a happy rural community in tune with nature, happily worshipping the sun. The second is based in the present, in the ruins of the city, stoned in order to forget, hoping it wasn't true, with just a glimmer of hope as the sun broke through. The third was a sci-fi-based theme of mankind, having destroyed the earth, being forced to flee in a spacecraft armada in order to set up home on another planet. The most moving line that recognises such damage is 'Look at Mother Nature on the run in the 1970s'.

The track was one of a number of environmental songs that Neil has written over the years. It sums up his affinity with nature and despair at the mess we are making of the world. The tone of the album was set.

'Only Love Can Break Your Heart' (Neil Young)

A sad song of heartbreak written for Graham Nash when he was very down following the break-up of his relationship with Joni Mitchell.

Another Spartan production, with Neil's slow-strummed acoustic to the fore and other instrumentation unobtrusively deployed for emphasis or support. Neil's strained and anguished falsetto provides the suitable emotional impact for this epitome of sadness. Not that the track is gloomy; the wafting melody is far too good to allow it to descend into gloom. 'Someone should call him and see if he can come out. Try to lose the down that he's found'. That line always seemed to optimistically suggest that the despair would end sometime and friends would rally around.

However, I am sure that this song also is about Neil's own romantic ventures. He'd certainly suffered his share of heartache. His first marriage to Susan Acevedo (his cinnamon girl hostess), with whom he had gotten married in the same cabin where they were recording the album, had ended in divorce that very year. No doubt his heart was broken, too. 'But only love can break your heart. Try to be sure right from the start. Yes, only love can break your heart. What if your world should fall apart?'

'Southern Man' (Neil Young)

This controversial song is the centrepiece of the album for me – a heartfelt song about racism in the Deep South that Neil sings with deep fury. This is one of the tracks that gets as near as anything to the improvisation and grungy rock of *Everybody Knows This Is Nowhere*. Except this isn't Crazy Horse. Instead of feeding off Danny Whitten's riffing guitar, Neil is extemporising off of, and around, Nils Lofgren's piano riff. Danny, along with Stephen Stills, is only there on the backing vocals. Ralph Molina is there on that heavy, persistent drumbeat, but the bass is Greg Reeves.

Despite the bad back, Neil gives full vent to his electric guitar improvisations. In the instrumental passages, Neil lets fly with the full fury of his stabbing notes, angry chords and staccato bursts of repeating notes that sound like snarling machine gun fire. He attacks his guitar with real venom, straining and forcing sounds to express his anger, as the band churn away on their circular, heavy pattern and Nils Lofgren lays down that repeating piano coda. We're well away from the high falsetto now and into Neil's full-throated rage. He's holding nothing back. And there's Danny coming in with able support on the chorus. All the ingredients boil together to produce a fine gumbo of heavy rock.

Lyrically, the song is every bit as strong as the sound. We're dealing with the endemic racism of the Southern States, with their violent repression of the African American population and history of slavery. He's going for it full tilt, citing the Ku Klux Klan and burning crosses, as well as the hypocrisy of Christianity and sexual indiscretions. Neil is asking the question: 'How long? How long? How long?' This is the 20th century; the world has changed. Racism is not to be tolerated. The Southern racist mentality is going to change too and soon – 'Southern change gonna come at last, now your crosses are burning fast. Southern man'.

The no-holds-barred approach received a lot of criticism from some Southerners. Lynyrd Skynyrd produced a scathing attack on Neil in their song 'Sweet Home Alabama', which was aimed at both 'Southern Man' and 'Alabama' (from the *Harvest* album). Neil acknowledged their sentiments and claimed that the song was really just aimed at 'Alabama', which deserved their criticism because it was so condescending. He claimed to have really dug the Lynyrd Skynyrd song.

When Neil gets the bit between his teeth, as on tracks like this and 'Ohio', there is no room for compromise. It's a full-hearted attack on what he perceives to be wrong. Works for me.

'Till The Morning Comes' (Neil Young)

How can you follow a track as powerful as 'Southern Man'? Easy. You produce a one-minute 17-second song telling everyone you want change NOW! No waiting. You've just got until the morning and that new day to bring that change around.

Nils comes in, playing the melody on piano. Neil sings the first stanza in a low register as the rhythm section enters. The vocal repeats and then the flugelhorn repeats the melody. Finally, Neil reverts to falsetto, with backing from Stephen Stills and Danny Whitten. 'I'm gonna give you/Till the morning comes, till the morning comes'. Unfortunately, it has been 53 years and that morning has been slow in coming!

'Oh Lonesome Me' (Don Gibson)

Side two opens in more of the same downward mood, as the full band perform this country-flavoured, doom-laden song of unrequited love, written in the 1950s by Don Gibson. In many ways, it is quite out of step with the music of the time, though Dylan has already gone down that country road and The Eagles and Jackson Browne are on the horizon. The times they were a-changin'.

The song, recorded with Crazy Horse at an earlier session, starts with a slow strummed guitar and an aching harmonica, melancholy piano and a slow dirge of a vocal. Neil normally sings songs like this in his strangled falsetto, but not this time. This is his lower register, all weighed down with misery. The instrumentation is precise and clear. There is even a burst of Neil's electric guitar towards the end.

Is this a glimpse into his mental state following the break-up with Susan Acevedo? This should have been a real downer, except that the exceptional melody and brilliance of performance create a real earworm of a cover of Don Gibson's country standard. Once again, Neil transforms it into something more.

The track was released as a single prior to the album coming out.

'Don't Let It Bring You Down' (Neil Young)

From those first two ominous chords, you think you might be in for a dose of depression, but this is really a song of optimism and hope. 'Don't let it bring you down. It's only castles burning. Find someone who's turning and you will come around'. Neil leads us through the pits of this uncaring modern world with an 'Old man lying by the side of the road with the lorries rolling by' and 'Dead man lying by the side of the road with the daylight in his eyes', but is telling us that there are better days ahead. We have to find the ones who really care, who are turning against the madness, and we can create something better. There is a better way.

Neil sings this song of hope in his wispy high falsetto, giving it all the force he can muster, as the band settle into an easy, chunky, steady rhythm. The poetic lyrics bleed out of his spirit. No matter how bad things are, they are going to get better. The raw emotion is cradled in that unique voice. The bass bubbles up from below. The song slows, then builds. The backing drops out to almost nothing and it tapers off into thin air.

The intensity, poetry and meticulous craft make this very special.

'Birds' (Neil Young)

A solo piano with a simple motif, Neil's voice soft and gentle, Crazy Horse coming in on backing vocals for the chorus – such a straightforward arrangement, but so effective because the performance is so meticulously carried out and so heartfelt. It conveys a wealth of feeling. Not so much a break-up song as a eulogy.

He may be saying that he's going, he's leaving her behind wounded and devastated, but he's telling her that it will all work out; it's going to be alright. There will be another love just as bright in the future. It will be even better. 'Tomorrow see the things that never come today'.

'When You Dance I Can Really Love' (Neil Young)

From the sublime to the outrageous. Neil is going for a lifting of spirits with a track as polar opposite to the emotional weight of the previous song. Where that was the epitome of delicacy and exposed emotion, this is visceral, straight from and to the gut.

We're back to the full intensity of those Crazy Horse riffs, the full-throttle grunge before there was grunge. Neil is releasing it all. 'When you dance, do your senses tingle? Then, take a chance. In a trance, while the lonely mingle with circumstance'. Takes me straight back to the mid-sixties, crazy dancing with my crazy girl, lost in that trance. Back to that primitive spirit that created that first rock 'n' roll revolution in the 1950s. Dancing is primitive. It taps back into the tribal instinct, with drums pounding around that fire. We're still there. This takes us there. Let yourself go and get lost in the trance.

The track kicks off with riffing guitars playing a simple but powerful sequence of chords – D G C Bbm Dm and F. The drumming is superb, right on the money, and the bass throbs and then riffs with real power, adding another dimension that sets the tone. The guitar is dirty and aggressive – this is what rock 'n' roll should sound like. The instrumental exchanges are immense, so powerful. Danny Whitten was not in good shape but still managed to pull this bravura performance out of nowhere. Turn the volume right up and they vibrate through your viscera. Nils is also in there on the keyboard; you can hear him at times. On top of all that, you have Neil using his voice like an incantation, ably backed by the background chorus: 'Ooooohoooh I can really love!'

It feels like a steam train. Fall into it. Free your mind and allow your body to flow and jerk to this wall of sound. The spirit lives.

'I Believe In You' (Neil Young)

On this seesaw of an album, where Neil is playing with our emotions, aesthetics and gut, we are heading for another change as he slows things right down and goes country. The band create a slow guitar-based countrified rock sound to a solid drumbeat and sparsely spaced bass. Neil's voice is low and oozes with sincerity. The vocal rises in register and intensity for the hook, with the backing vocals adding to the mix. The guitars pick and strum together to create a sensual bed of notes and chords. There's a pause, then into the second verse. The piano is quite strident, as it builds towards the end and fades.

This was one of the tracks recorded with Crazy Horse before the Crosby, Stills, Nash & Young tour and Neil's rethink, another song of breaking up, this time with a rather condescending attitude. He's telling her he's leaving, he can't commit, he has no love in this one-sided love affair, but she's going to be fine. He believes in her.

If I was the woman in question, I'm not sure that I'd find that kind of appeasement very satisfactory, even if it is sung with great beauty and passion. The second verse is telling. He's unsure, but now just wants to be friends. It was nothing more than a fling, but even though he doesn't love her, he cares. They'll meet up and laugh about it at some future time. I'm not so sure.

'Cripple Creek Ferry' (Neil Young)

Now we're in for a jaunty, country ramble down Cripple Creek towards the apocalypse.

This was one of the songs Neil wrote for the *After The Gold Rush* film idea that never happened. The film was concerned with the end of the world, specifically with California disappearing in a great flood.

This song forms a picture in my head of one of those New Orleans paddle steamers pushing its way through the flooded undergrowth on its way to Armageddon. I'm not sure why the water's going down, though. The captain doesn't seem to know what's going on and the gambler is out to make a killing. There's no mention of the passengers, though. Took me a while to realise that this was after the apocalypse – hence the jaunty feel. The water was going down. These were the survivors. We were heading back to more of the same. Our leaders haven't a clue and the conmen line us up.

The music is one minute and 34 seconds of drum-driven country rock. Neil sings the verse and everyone comes in on the chirpy chorus. Sounds much too jolly to be sailing to doom. A bit like the Titanic. I wonder if that was in Neil's mind. More probably, it's jaunty because those waters are receding and we've got another chance. It certainly makes for a cheery sing-a-long ending to the album. Despite being totally at odds with everything that has gone before, it is yet another tune that works its way into your psyche.

Outtakes
'Wonderin'' (Neil Young)
The band set up a great lurching rhythm based around the slow drums, thumping bass notes and strummed guitars. There's a great piano jangling in the right-hand track. Neil's voice is soft and pensive. The female chorus repeats to the out. It's a simple love song. Neil's walking and wondering if she'll come home and be his lady. From the sound of it, that's doubtful. Susan Acevedo, maybe?

'Wonderin'' (alternate) (Neil Young)
This is a much more upbeat version, with a great jangly, fuzzed-up guitar and Neil's vocal much smoother and almost crooning. He's still wondering, but he sounds much happier on this version. It has more of a pop feel to it. On the fade out, instead of the girl chorus, we are treated to Danny Whitten repeating 'knowing that I need you to save me' in response to Neil's 'I'm wondering', before they fade out with a series of 'aaah aaah's.

The track was later given a delightful Doo-Wop treatment on Neil's fabulous retro rock 'n' roll/R&B 1983 outing *Everybody's Rockin'*.

'Birds' (Neil Young)
This is the full electric band version that was released as the B-side of the 'Only Love Can Break Your Heart' single.

Nothing can disguise the beauty of the melody. The electric guitar interaction creates a gentle folk-rock vibe. The drums produce a slow, steady metronomic pace. The bass is superb in its understated throb, augmenting the busy guitars. Overall, a bright folk rock vibe is created. Neil's voice exudes his feelings, but, for me, does not reach the intensity or delicate nuance that he does so well on the stark LP piano version.

Singles
'Only Love Can Break Your Heart' b/w 'Birds'
This used to be a collector's item because, although the A-side 'Only Love Can Break Your Heart' was lifted straight off the album, the B-side 'Birds' was the electric band version that could not be found anywhere else. Of course, now it has been included on the CD as an outtake. This only reached a miserable 33 in the US charts and failed to score in the UK.

'When You Dance I Can Really Love' b/w 'Sugar Mountain' (non-album version)
Once again, Neil has paired the title track from the album, 'When You Dance I Can Really Love', with a non-album track on the B-side. This time, 'Sugar Mountain', the non-album track, has already been released as the B-side of 1969's 'The Loner' and 1970's 'Cinnamon Girl'. Despite receiving a lot of airplay and being a great track, this only climbed to number 93 on the US charts and got nowhere in the UK.

Guest Appearances

Stephen Stills auditioned for The Monkees but failed to get in because his hair and teeth were not considered photogenic enough. However, it did set up a connection and Michael Nesmith was a friend and huge early fan of Buffalo Springfield. That relationship meant that when they felt they needed a bit of musical assistance, they called up Neil Young to put some oomph in the studio.

'As We Go Along' (King, Stern)
From the Soundtrack album *Head* by The Monkees
Release Date: 1968
Written by Carole King and Toni Stern, supposedly when they were in their early teens, this psychedelic ballad was sung by Mickey Dolenz in his best Grace Slick impersonation. Neil can be heard adding the electric guitar to the mix.

    Head was a satirical movie written by Jack Nicholson while on LSD, following a marijuana-assisted session brainstorming into a microphone with The Monkees and Bob Rafelson. That kind of explains the mad plot and antics. Nicholson and Dennis Hopper both make cameo appearances. The Monkees provided the soundtrack.

'You And I' (Jones, Chadwick)
From the album *Instant Replay* by The Monkees
Release Date: 1969
Neil added the edgy lead guitar (and some backing vocal) to this rockin' Monkees tune. Davy Jones takes the vocal on this story of The Monkees. They came, they grew and they will shortly be replaced. The message is that a pretty face only lasts a short while.

Live Albums

Sugar Mountain – Live At Canterbury House 1968

Personnel:

Neil Young: guitar, vocals

Producer: Neil Young

Archivist: Joel Bernstein

Engineer: Harry Sitam

Assistant engineer: John Hausmann

Recorded at Canterbury House Ann Arbor, MI on 9 and 10 November 1968

Chart Positions: UK: 72, US: 40

This is a flawless compilation of the two gigs Neil performed at the small Canterbury House, Ann Arbor, Michigan. It captures Neil at his best in a small, warm and friendly venue. The banter with the audience shows the relaxed atmosphere. Even while laying the groundwork for a rocky album with Crazy Horse, he was showing how much his acoustic guitar playing had matured and gave full rein to that fragile, anguished voice with its deceptive strength. The songs sound incredibly well-honed, with definite performances of old songs such as 'Nowadays Clancy Can't Even Sing' that wrested them back from Buffalo Springfield's elaborations. This is the gig that 'Sugar Mountain' was lifted from and used as the B-side on three later singles.

The album is a snapshot of Neil just starting out on his solo career, pretty much putting a new career together from scratch. Although he had his reputation from his time in Buffalo Springfield, as a solo artist, he was an unknown quantity. People were blasé about members of bands going solo. Mostly, it proved to be a mediocre disappointment. The solo performers, often overconfident and buoyed up by ego, proved to be a pale shadow of the band. Would Neil prove to be any better? Neil, at the best of times, seemed to be the strange one in the band, hanging back in the shadows, with his tasselled buckskin jacket, and, despite Buffalo's success and hype and the exceptional quality of their material, they never repeated that early success with 'For What It's Worth' and were commercially largely a spent force.

The other thing of note was that he actually did not have a great number of songs behind him at this time. He was putting the debut album together, had his Buffalo Springfield tracks and that was about it.

This is Neil flying by the seat of his pants. Remember, he'd tried this once before and fallen flat on his face. Now, with more experience, more craft and more good songs, the question remained as to whether he could make a go of it. That must have been nerve-racking, but Neil did not seem to be consumed by nerves or any lack of confidence. He was a risk-taker.

From the Emcee's introduction, it seems that more people turned up than expected. That says something. But here, Neil is booked into a small venue with free food and they are not expecting to sell it out.

On the first number, Neil's vocal starts off sounding frail, but he soon settles into his usual emotive pattern – the strummed guitar creating an interesting repeating refrain. We can feel it now. The between-song banter is relaxed. He's going to let his hair grow and grow. That's what we did back then. We didn't all buy 1934 Bentleys, though – which is what he did with the residuals. He goes on to explain how 'Mr. Soul' only took five minutes to write and tells us that the song just came to him out of nowhere. I remember Arlo Guthrie saying something like that, too. He said it was like fishing for songs from the aether – and you did not want to be downstream of Bob Dylan. The version of 'Mr. Soul' is slightly wavery, with some choppy guitar that does not carry the gravitas of the Buffalo Springfield electric version. He wasn't doing the trick of disaster, though. It holds up. It's always good to hear these stripped-down versions, even if they don't always measure up. At this point, he tells the audience that these were being recorded. It's quite unusual to have a proper recording from this time. We're fortunate that they did. I don't know how he pulled that off.

He delivers the Buffalo Springfield classic 'Expecting To Fly' with a vulnerable charm that suits the song and lays bare the beauty of the melody. That vulnerability extends through 'Last Trip To Tulsa', with the frailty of the vocal seeming to add to the delivery, giving the song an ethereal touch. In the rap that follows, he recounts the story of how he worked for two weeks at Coles bookstore in Toronto. He was fired for irregularity. He was taking speed, so some days, he was on the ball. Some days, he could not be bothered.

The acoustic version of 'The Loner' feels instrumentally insipid and doesn't stack up against the electric version on the debut album, although the strum pattern is rather unique. We then get some story about how he used to play lead guitar in a blues band. Was he thinking of The Mynha Birds here? It's not clear.

Moving on to 'Birds', we find a gentle acoustic arrangement that really does work. The emotion is brimming and the soft delivery suits the content. The song was not going to be released until *After The Gold Rush* and then as a piano piece, but this amply demonstrates that it would have been just as effective in a guitar-based arrangement.

At this point, Neil is caught in indecision about what to play and plays an excerpt from 'Winterlong' before abandoning that and moving on to a reedy version of 'Out Of My Mind'. Neil explains how he wrote the song before any of the success with the band had happened. It's a druggy excursion, a play on words, through the perils of fame taking you out of your mind. Strange to think that it was written before there was any such fame. This acoustic version sounds more like a lament, but the dreamy arrangement works.

Moving on to 'If I Could Have Her Tonight', we are into another new song. This doesn't work anywhere near as well for me as the album version. It sounds too hesitant. Neil is still learning and developing it. However, from the audience's reaction, it sounds as if they appreciated it. But then, they hadn't heard the album yet. Then, after a snatch of 'Classical Gas', we're on to a great version of 'Sugar Mountain'. Neil doesn't tell us much, other than he wrote

'Sugar Mountain' about five years earlier and hasn't sung it for four and a half years – even though that's not strictly true. The song was written when he was playing solo in the folk clubs and so is ideally suited for this setting. It works perfectly. So much so that this is the version that was subsequently used as the B-side on no less than three singles (including 'Heart Of Gold'). It's good to hear it here in context with the rest of the concert.

Neil is giving the audience a taste of what is to come by airing some of the new material. 'I've Been Waiting For You' is a number that will appear on the forthcoming debut album. It works well on the record, but it's interesting to hear it stripped down to its bare essentials.

After asking for requests, Neil launches into 'Nowadays Clancy Can't Even Sing'. This song sounds brilliant, but then it's been around for a long time by now and Neil has honed it into shape through both his solo folk days and electric Buffalo Springfield time. The simple solo acoustic arrangement brings out the melody and highlights those poetic lyrics.

By now, Neil is thoroughly relaxed and has the audience completely with him. He relates an amusing anecdote about running out on stage with Buffalo Springfield and playing out of tune to a teeny-bop audience. Then, he tells an amusing story of how he wrote 'The Old Laughing Lady' about four years before on a napkin in a restaurant while waiting for their car to be repaired after it had been wrecked. Then, he explains the song was put in D modal tuning before launching into the song, which works very well in this acoustic setting. The sparse arrangement emphasises the bleakness with some great guitar flourishes.

For the finale, Neil produces an intriguing acoustic version of the fragmentary 'Broken Arrow'. It is interesting to see how Neil has put together this arrangement of what was a Jack Nietche collage of sounds on the debut album. It works very well in both forms. The acoustic, live version is completely different and fascinating.

There are two bonus tracks: one is available on iTunes and the other is a hidden bonus track on the CD that I found almost impossible to find. The iTunes number is the well-established 'I Am A Child'. This is another of the classic Young tracks that he has honed into shape through repeated performances. It seems just as powerful in this format. The CD bonus track is not a piece of music but a short, hilarious anecdote called 'Number 1 Hit Record Rap'.

And that's it. We have a properly recorded live show from the very beginning of Neil's solo career, just as he was coming out of the blocks – even if it is culled from two separate shows. This is not only a historical document, but a worthy, extremely listenable album in its own right.

Tracklisting: 'Emcee intro', 'On The Way Home', 'Songwriting Rap', 'Mr. Soul', 'Recording Rap', 'Expecting To Fly', 'The Last Trip To Tulsa', 'Bookstore Rap', 'The Loner', 'I Used To... Rap', 'Birds', 'Winterlong' (excerpt), 'Out Of My Mind'

Intro, 'Out Of My Mind', 'If I Could Have Her Tonight', 'Classical Gas Rap' (Mason Williams/Young), 'Sugar Mountain Intro', 'Sugar Mountain', 'I've Been Waiting For You', 'Songs Rap', 'Nowadays Clancy Can't Even Sing', 'Tuning Rap', 'The Old Laughing Lady' Intro, 'The Old Laughing Lady', 'Broken Arrow', Bonus Tracks: 'I Am A Child' (iTunes-only bonus track) '#1 Hit Record Rap' (hidden MP3 bonus track)

Live At The Riverboat 1969

Personnel:
Neil Young: acoustic guitar and vocal
Produced by Neil Young
Release Date: 2 June 2009
All songs written by Neil Young
Chart positions: UK: did not chart, US: did not chart

This live performance was gleaned from three one-man shows performed at the Riverboat Coffee House in Toronto. It has never been released as a stand-alone disc but is part of the *Neil Young Archives Vol. 1: 1963–1972* box set released in June 2009. It is a great-quality recording of a seminal gig. This was Neil's first return to Toronto after having left to join Buffalo Springfield. At this stage in his career, although he had had a great deal of fame and exposure with the Buffalos, he was still an unknown quantity as a solo performer. Hence, he was playing in small venues. The coffee house would have drawn in people who remembered him with The Squires, as well as those who knew him from the Buffalos. They would have been interested to hear what he had to offer.

There was no hiding the voice now. In a solo acoustic setting, it was fully exposed, yet, following the beginning of his liaison with Crazy Horse, it feels as if Neil has come to terms with it at last. While, at times, it sounds frail, tender and anguished, about to crack, it carries an innocence and poignancy that makes it incredibly emotional and communicative. People can relate to this.

The beauty of the album is that it was a recording of gigs in an intimate setting. There is the close-up relationship with the audience, the talking and the asides. Because of his lack of success with singles and his debut album, he was not yet a big name. He was playing in a small venue, feet away from his audience and that makes for a very warm vibe.

The other interesting aspect of the gig is the setlist. He included material from both his Buffalo Springfield days, as well as songs from his debut album. It is wonderful to hear these tracks stripped down to their bare necessities, just Neil and an acoustic, without all the production. But, in truth, it is the banter that makes the recording special.

This is a historic moment in an extensive career, the start of that long journey. This is a record of how it was before fame hit and the big stadiums loomed. For two years, 1968-1970, Neil was approachable, close and personal. Never again.

This time, Neil starts off with an audience favourite – the coming-of-age 'Sugar Mountain'. Neil explains about the writing of the song and Joni Mitchell's 'Circle Game', the humorous ending acting as an ice-breaker. He sounds relaxed and the audience laugh. They're with him. The song is delivered in all its glory, plucked and strummed with Neil in his falsetto voice in a nigh-on perfect delivery.

After a strange, long tale of a visit to the doctor, with a weird report of the doctor putting his hand right inside him to sort out his problem, we get a song about death. 'The Old Laughing Lady' is delivered as a great live acoustic version, with a perfect balance and good dynamic. It starts with a plodding, strummed guitar and Neil speaks over the top, reporting that he has not washed his hair today, before launching into the song in a subdued, hushed tone. The guitar is very forceful between verses.

Neil moves on to his druggy song 'Flying On The Ground Is Wrong', with an intro about how the audience affect the performance and how singers began writing songs about dope – some kind of tribal thing. Then, to go along with the psychedelic experience, he explains how bands changed their names in order to be freaky. The acoustic arrangement works well, with that guitar almost singing the melody and Neil's wistful voice crooning slowly with feeling – another pared-back gem. It is so good to hear the song undressed.

For 'On The Way Home', Neil explains that it is a song about leaving friends before cutting loose with this emotive offering. Neil reflects on what he has left behind in order to follow his dream. It has the depth of feeling required. I love Richie Furay's voice, but the Buffalo Springfield version is too bright and breezy for such a sad, whimsical song. Neil's voice and slower arrangement suit it better.

After the interval, Neil starts with a plaintif 'I've Loved Her So Long'. I do love the highly produced version on that debut album, but this very basic version positively aches. He moves on to a delightful acoustic 'I Am A Child', with a strange introduction that explains that the song is in B minor if anybody wants to play along. He then asks if everyone knows who Allen A-Dale is and then claims that he's better than Clapton. I'm not quite sure if this fictional wandering minstrel, from the Robin Hood mythology, has anything to do with anything.

Following a couple of light-hearted fragments about bubble gum, he introduces Bruce Palmer and proceeds to deliver a near-perfect, seven-minute acoustic rendition of 'Last Trip To Tulsa' – a stoned trip through a newspaper on a car journey to Tulsa. I think this basic arrangement works as well, if not better than the album version.

Before playing a remarkable acoustic 'Broken Arrow', we have an intro about words. Neil examines how words like 'request' and 'disease' were invented. 'Request – quite a word. Re-quest, that's a good word'. 'We don't even think about what we're saying. Dis-ease – disease. Interesting'. Neil's fascination with the construction of words shows in his songwriting. Once again, this complex, multi-faceted song works as a solo version with just an acoustic guitar. Neil organises all the bridges perfectly. The changes in tempo and tone work well as he pulls together the dissimilar components into a cohesive structure.

'Whisky Boot Hill' just about makes the grade. Unfortunately, it can't compete with the fabulous version with Crosby, Stills, Nash & Young. The CSN&Y version is stellar; this is just good.

Before singing 'Expecting To Fly' as the finale, he confides about how he'd been uptight for two weeks about playing solo. Now, in this last set, he's so relaxed, he says he can hardly play. Nonetheless, he produces a near-perfect performance.

I know the performances were selected from sets from three separate days, but what stands out, for me, is the quality of this solo performance. The song arrangements and stage presence are all highly evolved. This is someone at the beginning who is already there.

Tracklisting: 'Emcee Intro'/'Sugar Mountain Intro', 'Sugar Mountain', 'Incredible Doctor Rap', 'The Old Laughing Lady', 'Audience Observation'/'Dope Song'/'Band Names Rap', 'Flying On The Ground Is Wrong', 'On The Way Home Intro', 'On The Way Home', 'Set Break'/'Emcee Intro', 'I've Loved Her So Long', 'Allen A-Dale Rap', 'I Am A Child', '1956 Bubblegum Disaster', 'The Last Trip To Tulsa', 'Words Rap', 'Broken Arrow', 'Turn Down The Lights Rap', 'Whiskey Boot Hill', 'Expecting To Fly Intro', 'Expecting To Fly'

Live At The Fillmore East
Personnel:
Neil Young: guitar, vocals
Danny Whitten: guitar, vocal
Billy Talbot: bass
Ralph Molina: drums, backing vocals
Jack Nitzsche: electric piano
Producer: Paul Rothchild
Recorded live on 6 and 7 March 1970 at the Fillmore East
Label: Reprise Label
Chart positions: UK: 88, US: 55
This was the Neil Young and Crazy Horse tour that supported the release of the *Everybody Knows This Is Nowhere* album. The band, at this time, featured the great Danny Whitten, who sadly died from an overdose two years later in 1972, on the eve of another tour. Apart from the stalwarts, Billy Talbot on bass and Ralph Molina on drums, it also featured Jack Nitzsche on electric piano.

This was the band that enabled Neil to really let fly. They not only provided a solid base for him to work off but also seemed to intuitively accommodate his flights of fancy, improvisations and idiosyncrasies. This was raw, naked power unleashed and you could hear that they all revelled in it. David Crosby supposedly ridiculed Talbot and Molina for not being sophisticated enough. They weren't. Sophistication wasn't their thing. They were downright mean and dirty. Just what Neil wanted.

The other aspect that stands out is how together they were. These songs had been honed into shape through hundreds of hours of playing together. All those days sitting around in a circle playing for fun, rehearsing the act to knock everything into shape, really paid off. They were so incredibly tight that they could be loose.

The album of the show was finally released in 2006 and features all the songs from the electric set (they also did an acoustic set – as yet unreleased), except for 'Cinnamon Girl', which Neil considered to be out of tune. 'Cinnamon Girl' was eventually released as a Blu-ray download in his *Archives* series – so still not easy to find.

'Everybody Knows This Is Nowhere' sets the tone. Right from the start, the bass and drums power through as a solid spine that everything hangs off. The balance of the recording is perfect. All the instruments and vocals come through clearly at just the right level. Neil and Danny's sparring guitars are great, with those scissoring riffs cutting across. Neil's vocal is strong and Danny's high-pitched backing vocals give it that energy. You can even hear Ralph doing his vocal bit too. Everything blends perfectly. A superb live rendition and a great way to get the live album off the ground. That power is continued into the less familiar 'Winterlong'. This unreleased song, with Neil pining for love, was eventually released on the *Decades* compilation. Although slower, it still revolves around that same thundering rhythm section. Neil and Danny's guitars merge with some lyrical guitar runs. The jerky guitar exchanges and rolling melody circle, build and fall to create a changing, edgy dynamic. Danny shares the vocals with Neil, and towards the end, there is a call-and-response section.

'Down By The River' allows the band to demonstrate their power. They show why Neil selected them. It's not about musicianship but rather raw energy and intuitive jamming. Stephen Stills was appalled by them, but Neil recognised that they unleashed freedom in his playing. He relished their crudity. Danny Whitten's short, dirty, strummed intro summons the band in and they plunge straight into some of the dirtiest garage rock ever. The rhythm section sets up a pounding refrain for the others to work off, thudding through the belly for 12 and a half minutes of primordial rock. This is a nuclear meltdown of instruments, with Neil's voice dark and sinister and Danny's underpinning it. The first verse sets the tone: is this a murder or a break-up? No, it's definitely murder on this live version! It's too violent to be a break-up. The guitar riffs and builds into a scorching solo as Neil lets fly with an endless series of stabbing notes.

The next verse is full of sorrow. Neil tells us he's being dragged over that rainbow. His dreams are shattered. Another solo begins as the band set up a repeating refrain, with wandering bass, steady drums and Danny's slashing chords. Neil's guitar builds with a stuttering machine gun fire of blazing notes before becoming more lyrical. This raw guitar soloing is both unique and highly experimental. He is creating a totally new style based not so much on technique as inspiration.

After that thundering start, Neil cools things down with a countrified version of 'Wondering'. Although Neil announced that this delightful song was from his next album, it would not see the official light of day until it was given the Doo-Wop treatment on the Shocking Pinks album *Everybody's Rockin'* in 1983. It's a departure from the hard, garage rock, with a more melodic country rock feel, easy flowing, sweet and breezy, more like the restrained sophistication of *Buffalo Springfield*. The picked guitar sounds bell-like and clean. Towards the end, it has a fabulous call-and-response section, which sounds like it's Billy Talbot.

After that brief chill, the energy picks up again with a rockin' version of 'Come On Baby Let's Go Downtown'. This was later edited by the great Richard Berry and released on the 1975 album *Tonight's The Night*. We're back to the garage grunge. 'Snake eyes, French fries and I got lots of gas'. That's Danny Whitten on the main vocal, with Neil in the support role. We're heading downtown to have a good time – it's heavy: 'They'll be selling stuff when the moon begins to rise'. The band are rollicking and Danny is on the ball. It's such a shame that things got too heavy. Danny was getting into the hard drugs and becoming addicted to heroin – that kind of stuff kills. Yet, this track, which typifies Danny as he was before the monkey got him, is so full of life, energy and fun. The irony is that it is a requiem for Danny. He went downtown too many times.

'Cowgirl In The Sand' is a masterclass in unleashed improvisation. This is the absolute consummate recording of a fabulous song – 16 minutes of undiluted bliss. A few scratchy chords to set the beat and the band thunder in like a stampede of elephants, with Neil's searing guitar stinging over the top. The bass cooks like molten lava, holding it all together, the relentless beat kicking into the gut. It's full throttle all the way, careering into the mystic due to a blistering three-way binge with Jack's electric piano and the two guitars. This is probably one of the best guitar solos of all time. Neil is, at times, frenzied, frantic, lost in the music, out of control, yet right there, improvising a stream of licks that flow lyrically, rising and falling, with notes sometimes sharp and stinging, and at other times, extended and wailing like a demented banshee. You don't want this to end. The imagination is unleashed into free fall as that rhythm section holds it together while Neil extemporises. The bits out of the mouth and the reins have been dropped as Neil pours his inner passions through the strings of that guitar. He's on fire. When, towards the end of this never-ending lick, the verse finally re-emerges, it brings it all back down to earth. Never have 16 minutes passed so quickly.

'Cinnamon Girl', the final track – and one of my favourites – was left off this album because Neil wasn't satisfied with the performance. He thought it was out of tune. Consequently, it was relegated to a Blu-Ray download on *Archives*.

I don't know about being out of tune. If you want power and passion, you go for this every day. Give me rawness over sophistication. This is garage rock at its most powerful. It sets the hairs rising, heart pounding and blood singing. As soon as the band come crashing in with those evil riffs and pounding backbeat, you're on your feet!

Tracklisting: 'Everybody Knows This Is Nowhere' (Neil Young), 'Winterlong' (Neil Young), 'Down By The River' (Neil Young), 'Wonderin'' (Neil Young), 'Come On Baby Let's Go Downtown' (Neil Young, Danny Whitten), 'Cowgirl In The Sand' (Neil Young), 'Cinnamon Girl'

Live At The Cellar Door

Personnel:
Neil Young: vocal, guitar, piano
Produced: Neil Young and Henry Lewy
Recorded at The Cellar Door Club in Washington, DC on 30 November, 1 December and 2 December 1970
Label: Reprise Records
Chart positions: UK: 57, US: 28

Amazingly, eight months on from the full-throttle performances with Crazy Horse, rockin' the Fillmore, Neil was back in the small, intimate confines of a small 163-seater club for a six-night residency. It couldn't have been more different. It appears that part of the attraction for Neil was that they provided him with a nine-foot Steinway piano.

On the face of it, there is nothing much new to hear in this set. We have most of this solo material in similar concerts, except for the strange, unique piano arrangements on half of the material and the quiet, reverential silence of the performances. Most of the banter has been excised, so we don't get the warmth and humour of the exchanges within that intimate setting, but we do get a feel of a change in the relationship. Neil is now held in awe. He is relaxed and master of the stage and his tremulous voice commands the songs. He even manages a very stoned giggle or two.

This set of concerts was part of the promotion for the *After The Gold Rush* album, hence the setlist. The small club setting suited this very subdued, contemplative collection of songs. The introspective *Gold Rush* material lends itself to this melancholy vibe.

As he peers over the edge into a very different decade, the dream fading away, this is a very different Neil Young to the one singing these same songs a year or two back. This guy has come of age, even as the era that spawned him writhes in its death throes.

'Tell Me Why' is a powerful, confident start. An upbeat number, the guitar rings through strongly with a lot of bottom end. Neil means to set the tone. This has authority. Neil is sailing his heart through choppy waters in search of love. He is old enough to know what it's about, but still young enough to want to pay the price. Although still retaining that vulnerable waver, his vocal is full of power. With 'Only Love Can Break Your Heart', Neil is totally relaxed, with a slow, strongly strummed guitar oozing melancholy. The vocal still exudes the same authority but is more vulnerable. The hurt shows in the guitar work, as he expertly manoeuvres his way through the changes of tempo and chords.

His first foray on the Steinway is a rarity, as he produces a keyboard version of 'After The Goldrush'. He claims to have only been playing the piano seriously for one year, but it sounds good on this faithful piano rendition of the title track on the album.

'Expecting To Fly', the old Buffalo Springfield number, also gets the piano treatment. The forceful, crashing piano chords at the end of each verse are juxtaposed against Neil's anguished, frail voice. The piano arrangement creates a completely different-sounding song to the one we are used to.

'Bad Fog Of Loneliness' takes us back to the guitar for this almost-perfect, melancholic ramble through lonely days, with only dreams of that sweet caress. The song itself is another rarity. It fits in very nicely with the type of material that would end up on the *After The Gold Rush* and *Harvest* albums. The riff is similar to that in 'The Needle And The Damage Done' and the time changes in the bridge, from 4/4 time to 3/4 time, is the same as he uses in 'Words'. Indeed, it was recorded in 1971 during the *Harvest* sessions, using the same musicians – Ben Keith on steel guitar, Tim Drummond on bass and Kenny Buttrey on drums, with James Taylor and Linda Ronstadt on backing vocals. From the sound of it, that would have nestled well on the *Harvest* album. For some reason, it never made the cut and only later appeared on *Archives: Vol. 1.*

The new material keeps coming. 'Old Man' won't appear until *Harvest*. This was an extremely prolific period for Neil, with three very different albums coming out in quick succession. Here he is at a concert to promote the third of them and already looking forward to the next album. This is a run-out for this new song and it does sound like a run-through. He hasn't quite developed it with the authority he would have later. The song is brilliant and the arrangement is all there, but the performance sounds a tad subdued, as if he has not yet quite absorbed it into his DNA.

The piano arrangement perfectly suits 'Birds', a delicate song of leaving. It is probably the best version anywhere. The voice feels completely naked so that the nuance of the emotion is exposed. It aches with pain. 'Don't Let It Bring You Down' is also a consummate near-perfect performance of this song from *After The Gold Rush*. Somehow, with just a guitar, Neil manages to flesh it out into a fuller production.

Neil returns to that Steinway for an immaculate rendition of a most melancholy song of fate: 'See The Sky About To Rain'. Somehow, the piano doesn't fill all the space and so allows the poetic beauty of the lyrics to stand out in all their glory. Neil's voice always has that tremulous edge on these solo efforts, conveying a wealth of emotion. On this, the piano passage towards the end really adds to the piece. The song won't make a recorded appearance until the 1974 *On The Beach* album. It's bursting with words that are subject to different interpretations.

He stays on that Steinway for what is a unique piano rendition of 'Cinnamon Girl'. Nothing can ever beat that rousing, heavy guitar riffing that Crazy Horse unleash. But then, this isn't a competition. If it was just another version of the same arrangement, it would have nothing else to offer – this does. I never thought I'd ever hear a solo piano version. This doesn't come near to stirring me in the same way, but then it is great to have such a completely different arrangement. One has to view it as a different song. As such, it's a welcome addition. Neil likes experimenting. He said: 'That's the first time I've ever performed that song on piano!' and probably the last.

'I Am A Child' is honed to perfection and much the same as ever, but 'Down By The River' is a revelation. This smooth,, acoustic version is almost unrecognisable from the heavy, edgy Crazy Horse number. This starts off gentle and soothing, diametrically opposed to the vibe on the album. The arrangement brings out the hopeless fears, fraught worries, sadness and uncertainties of relationships with all their high emotions, jealousies and pain. Where the sheer power of Crazy Horse made this a possibility for a murder, this rendition is very much about a hot-headed split, a row, a brutal breakup. I know which version I prefer, but it's nice to have them both.

After toying with Crazy Horse, Neil turns his attention to Buffalo Springfield with a version of 'Flying On The Ground Is Wrong'. In the beginning, Neil starts playing around with the strings on the Steinway, creating a lot of sounds that make him chuckle in a stoned manner. He mutters, 'You'd laugh too if this is what you did for a living', which produces a laugh from the audience. He then goes on to explain that the song is essentially about dope. Back in the sixties, there were basically two kinds of people: those that were hip and those that weren't. It was a fundamental division. Marijuana was a shared sacrament, a symbol of being part of the scene. Smoking dope was a sign of the mental changes that had taken place and the rifts it provoked. This is a song about breaking up with his girlfriend Pam. She finds it hard to understand that Neil is moving into a different world now and she, not wanting to make that jump, is being left behind. The simple piano arrangement not only brings out the beauty of the melody but also lays bare the content of the lyrics, making it easier to assimilate. Neil tried to explain his feeling on this in an interview with *Uncut* magazine in 2012. He was basically saying that you had to be true to yourself and make the changes that are right for you. Sometimes that's hard; you hurt people and have to leave them behind as you move on: 'You can't worry about what people think. I never do. I never did, really'.

Tracklisting: 'Tell Me Why' (Neil Young), 'Only Love Can Break Your Heart' (Neil Young), 'After The Gold Rush' (Neil Young), 'Expecting To Fly' (Neil Young),

'Bad Fog Of Loneliness' (Neil Young), 'Old Man' (Neil Young), 'Birds' (Neil Young), 'Don't Let It Bring You Down' (Neil Young), 'See The Sky About To Rain' (Neil Young), 'Cinnamon Girl' (Neil Young), 'I Am A Child' (Neil Young), 'Down By The River' (Neil Young), 'Flying On The Ground Is Wrong' (Neil Young)

Conclusion
I can see why Neil liked the idea of doing these low-key gigs. The idea of having a Steinway at his disposal, to play about with, must have turned him on. Here he was, at the end of the sixties, in charge of his destiny and confidently striding into the next decade – this gig marks a transition. Just four weeks later, in January 1971, he performed the fabulous solo 2,600 seater Massey Hall gig with a totally different vibe.

Neil Young Compilation And Film Albums
Journey Through The Past
Featuring recordings from 1966-1971
Producers: Neil Young, L.A. Johnson
Label: Reprise
Release Date: 1972
Chart positions: UK: 46, US: 43

This double album is a soundtrack to the film of the same name. It features early material from Buffalo Springfield, Crosby, Stills, Nash & Young and solo Neil Young (as well as an assortment of other material). The soundtrack also works as a retrospective of Neil Young's work up until this period, which was then superseded by the 1977 release of *Decade*. It is especially significant for this book, as it includes a lot of his work in the sixties.

The film documentary is an idiosyncratic journey through a very selective past. Rather than taking a standard, mainstream approach using the regular recordings, it revolves around rarer TV concert appearances and outtakes. The highlights are a live version of 'Ohio' and a 16-minute version of 'Words'. It is a bizarre glimpse into the mind of Neil grappling with the music business and real life – at times, coherent; at others, extremely random. It was a film seen by the suits at Warner Brothers as being incoherent and uncommercial. They wouldn't have anything to do with it. The film is now included on the *Archives* box set.

It makes for a real glimpse into the past and one that probably ended Carrie Snodgrass's career as she puffed away on a jay. Hollywood promptly terminated her contract.

All songs written by Neil Young, except where noted.

'For What It's Worth/Mr. Soul' (Stills/Young) – Buffalo Springfield
This was a medley taken from studio recordings for the television program *The Hollywood Palace* put out on 20 January 1967. The recording here is a rare alternative version of 'Mr. Soul'. They mimed to the track for the broadcast. The version of Mr. Soul used here is an alternative mix to that used on *Buffalo Springfield Again* and cannot be remixed as the master tape was lost.

'Rock & Roll Woman' (Stills) – Buffalo Springfield
This track comes from a 1967 appearance on a TV special, *Popendipity*. It was recorded in the Warwick Musical Theatre on 16 November 1967.

'Find The Cost Of Freedom' – Crosby, Stills, Nash & Young
'Ohio' – Crosby Stills, Nash & Young
'Southern Man' – Crosby Stills, Nash & Young
These are live recordings by Crosby Stills, Nash & Young from the Fillmore East on 5 June 1970.

'Are You Ready For The Country' – Neil Young
'Alabama' – Neil Young
These are outtakes from the *Harvest* album recorded in sessions from
September 1971 with the Stray Gators. It was recorded at Neil's ranch in La
Honda, California.

'Let Me Call You Sweetheart' (Leo Friedman, Beth Slater)
An old 1910 song that was a big hit in 1911 for The Peerless Quartet. The
saccharine sweet number was added to The Library Of Congress National
Recording Registry in 2015 due to its cultural, historical and aesthetical
significance. It was selected because of the mood it espoused.

'Words (Between The Lines Of Age)' – Neil Young
This is an outtake from the Harvest album recorded in sessions from
September 1971 with the Stray Gators. It was recorded at Neil's ranch
in La Honda, California. It's a long 15-minute jam in the barn. The song
was written in response to the large retinue of folk that Carrie Snodgrass
brought with her to Neil's ranch. They took over, dominated, stole his peace
and made him paranoid. He once jumped out of the window to escape
them.
   Neil explained the meaning behind 'Words' to *Rolling Stone*:

'Words' is the first song that reveals a little of my early doubts about being
in a long-term relationship with Carrie. It was a new relationship. There
were so many people around all the time, talking and talking, sitting in a
circle smoking cigarettes in my living room. Words – too many of them,
it seemed to me. I was young and not ready for what I had gotten myself
into. I became paranoid and aware of mind games others were trying to
play on me.

The track starts off with some heavy, chunky guitar and sublime piano, as
Jack Nitzsche duets with Neil. Meanwhile, Tim Drummond's bass throbs and
Kenny Buttrey's drums set up a steady, shuffling beat to create a cyclical
groove, over which Neil lays out his lead. An ethereal pedal steel from Ben
Keith completes the picture. It has an interesting time signature of 11/8
between verses, reverting to 4/4 for verses and chorus, which gives it a
musical sophistication that propels it out of the norm. Neil's guitar gives a
blast of anger after he sings 'words'. Neil stops the recording to direct the
band into a slightly slower, more mellow groove that persists for 15 minutes,
with some variations in pace and timbre.

'Soldier' – Neil Young
This is the only new song from Neil on the album. It was actually recorded
in a sawmill. The noise in the background is the roar of the sawdust burner.

It later appeared, in edited form, on Neil's *Decade* compilation. As Neil explained to Jimmy McDonough in *Shakey*:

'Soldier' was written to represent the subconscious of the Graduate guy (a character in the film) movin' through his decision-making process about what he was going to do with his life or the kind of person he was going to be. That was the decision – to go either to drugs, to religion or the army.

It's a solo piano piece, slightly muffled in production. The song starts with heavy piano riffs and Neil sings in a high register, his voice very pure without a hint of his customary waver. Towards the end, there are some delicately picked notes.

The lyrics are very simple, and yet, reveal little. They are very difficult to interpret. 'Soldier, your eyes, they shine like the sun, I wonder why'. The soldier is the purveyor of death, yet light connotes life. Then, he says he saw Jesus walking on the river, but he couldn't deliver right away. He wonders why. Neil professes to have a spiritual view but is very sceptical about religion. He sees it all too often used for power. That comes across in those simple lyrics.

Decade

Producers: Neil Young, Elliot Mazer, Tim Mulligan, David Briggs
Label: Warner Brothers
Release Date: 1977

This was a triple album retrospective of Neil's career up until this point (1977), an extremely ambitious, unprecedented move on behalf of Neil and the Warner Brothers label. At that time, triple albums were almost unheard of. The project was the start of what would later develop into the *Archives* collection. Neil has a desire to archive everything he does. Strangely, he is not precious about his work. Although meticulous and demanding in the production of his music – and known for ruthlessly cutting out musicians, bands and others involved in making that music – if he feels that it is no longer working, he allows some material out that is not perfect or clearly juvenilia, while perversely holding back other material on spurious grounds. It's a peculiarity of Neil's. He will abandon tracks or shelf whole albums because he feels they are not right, then, he releases an archive containing early recordings and material that is clearly not up to his own high standards. It is sometimes hard to fathom.

On *Archives*, Neil set out to catalogue his entire career, from the earliest efforts and rejected takes to the honed gems. He has said that the public can discern for themselves why a particular outtake was rejected. *Decade* was an early attempt at archiving. Because the medium was vinyl, the number of tracks, even on a triple album, was limited. If you tried to include more than 20 minutes per side, the quality of sound was compromised, and Neil is always hot on the quality of sound. So, even with a triple album, there were severe limitations. Ironically, given Neil's attitude to the sound quality of CDs and MP3s, it wasn't until the advent of the CD, with the ability to put a large number of tracks together, that it really became possible to create a fully comprehensive archive of an artist's work that could go out to the public.

Decade is not by any means a 'Best of' album. It is an attempt to put the tracks together in chronological order so that it was possible to make sense of his career. It contained a few rarities unavailable anywhere else at the time. Unfortunately, for this book, most of these rarities did not pertain to the sixties. *Decade* formed a template for the later box sets that have now come out in their profusion. This 1977 release is relevant to this tome on Neil's work in the 1960s because over half of it is concerned with his output during this decade.

An interesting aside is that when Neil brought this out, he included handwritten notes on each of the tracks.

All the tracks are either from albums that have already been reviewed or from albums outside of the remit of this book.

Crosby, Stills, Nash & Young

Crosby, Stills & Nash were a supergroup, risen, phoenix-like out of the ashes of three highly successful sixties bands – The Byrds, Buffalo Springfield and The Hollies. The Byrds were enormous. They'd started with their folk-rock jangly arrangements of Dylan and Seeger songs and gone on to psychedelia. In the process, they had aligned themselves with – and been integral in – the development of the counter-culture. David Crosby had been thrown out of The Byrds in 1967 at the time of the making of *The Notorious Byrd Brothers*. It had been coming for a long time. David Crosby was the rich kid who'd gate-crashed his way into The Byrds in the early days, audaciously joining them uninvited on stage. He was always incredibly extroverted, confident and outspoken, becoming difficult to work with as his ego grew. That brought him into conflict with the over-huge egos in The Byrds, namely Roger McGuinn and Chris Hillman (two of the other original members had already gone). There had always been conflict regarding the direction of the band and, particularly, which songs were recorded. Each individual was keen to get their own material on the albums and not so keen on anybody else's.

David had been getting heavily into the mid-sixties drug scene, which did not help matters with the band's internal politics. There were many disgruntled feuds. At the crucial Monterey Pop Festival (which had been a showcase for many bands with Hendrix, The Who, Otis Redding and Janis Joplin stealing the show), Crosby really exasperated the rest of The Byrds, firstly, by giving long, rambly monologues on LSD, JFK and politics, and even more infuriatingly by joining Buffalo Springfield on stage, filling in for the absent Neil Young.

The final straw came with the recording of *The Notorious Byrd Brothers*. The recording had not been going well. There was disagreement over material and direction. David claimed that none of the band were good enough musicians to play with him. For some reason, they took offence. David wanted to include one of his songs about a menage a trois called 'Triad'. The rest of the band wanted a Goffin and King number, 'Going Back'. Crosby thought it was too commercial and refused to sing on it. They refused to put 'Triad' on the album (Jefferson Airplane recorded it later), kicked him out of the band and put a cover photo of the band peering out of stables on the front cover. Crosby was presented as the arse-end of a horse.

Stephen Stills had been the mainstay of Buffalo Springfield and was a highly sought-after session man. As the writer of their huge hit 'For What It's Worth', he was a man with a lot of status in the West Coast acid rock scene.

Buffalo Springfield had split up due to internal wrangling, mainly between him and Neil Young, over material, direction and leadership. The subsequent lack of success hadn't helped. After increasing acrimonious relationships, personnel absences, drug issues, management problems, touring pressures and label problems, the band had fallen apart.

Graham Nash had been the driving force in the British pop group The Hollies. They had achieved a string of Top Ten hits, but Graham had become increasingly frustrated with the shallowness of their music. As the mid-sixties counter-culture scene began to take off, he wanted the band to develop, become more experimental, and produce more complex music with more mature themes. Under the influence of Dylan's songwriting, bands like The Beatles and The Who were developing more sophisticated songs, with adult-orientated content dealing with real issues. The London underground and West Coast scenes were taking off and Graham wanted to be in the thick of the action. He no longer wanted to be churning out pop songs. He wanted something with more substance. The rest of The Hollies seemed content the way they were and did not want to change. Graham began hanging out in L.A. and, eventually, that led to a parting of the ways.

Laurel Canyon was where it all happened, where the musicians hung out. There was a community living there, including Neil Young, Stephen Stills, Joni Mitchell, David Crosby, Frank Zappa and members of Love and The Doors. It was vibrant and creative. Musicians would party together, hang out, jam together, try out ideas and exchange views. Neil lived in a wood cabin in the neighbouring Topanga Canyon and was part of the scene.

It was while jamming together in Laurel Canyon that Crosby, Stills & Nash discovered that their voices blended into the most beautiful of harmonies. The band Crosby, Stills & Nash was born. Their first album was an enormous hit, but, for the second one, they asked Neil Young to augment their sound on the album, despite the level of acrimony between Stills and Young in Buffalo Springfield. Stephen and Dallas Taylor were driving to a Neil Young gig with Crazy Horse. In *Shakey*, Stephen said to Dallas: 'How would you feel about Neil joining the band?' Dallas replied: 'Wow! Great, but isn't that why the Springfield broke up?' Stephen concluded: 'Oh no, man. It's gonna be different this time. It'll be cool'.

Crosby, Stills, Nash & Young were subsequently born. They began work on *Déjà Vu*. It was so anticipated, that it chalked up advance sales of two million. They were up there with the biggest acts on the planet. 'Young's voice, guitar, composition and stage presence added elements of darkness and mystery to songs that had previously dripped a kind of saccharin sweetness', said *Rolling Stone* writer Langdon Winner.

Neil Young was a superstar. He had money. He could buy his cars. He also moved out of Topanga Canyon and bought a 140-acre ranch with a log cabin near San Francisco at Half Moon Bay in September 1970. The ranch cost him $340,000. He finally had somewhere to escape to, away from the madness, back to nature. The old custodian of the property stayed on to look after it. He became the subject of 'Old Man'.

Déjà Vu (1970)

Personnel:

David Crosby: vocals on all tracks except '4+20', rhythm guitar on 'Almost Cut My Hair', 'Woodstock', 'Déjà Vu', 'Country Girl' and 'Everybody I Love You'

Stephen Stills: vocals on all tracks except 'Almost Cut My Hair', guitars on all tracks except 'Our House', bass on 'Carry On', 'Teach Your Children' and 'Déjà Vu', keyboards on 'Déjà Vu' and 'Everybody I Love You', organ on 'Carry On' and 'Woodstock', piano on 'Helpless' and 'Country Girl', percussion on 'Carry On'

Graham Nash: vocals on all tracks except 'Almost Cut My Hair' and '4+20', piano on 'Woodstock' and 'Our House', harpsichord on 'Our House', organ on 'Almost Cut My Hair', rhythm guitar on 'Teach Your Children' and 'Country Girl', percussion on 'Carry On' and 'Country Girl', tambourine on 'Teach Your Children'

Neil Young: vocals on 'Helpless' and 'Country Girl', guitars on 'Almost Cut My Hair', 'Helpless', 'Woodstock' and 'Country Girl', harmonica, pipe organ and vibraphone on 'Country Girl', organ on 'Country Girl' and 'Everybody I Love You'

Greg Reeves: bass on 'Almost Cut My Hair', 'Helpless', 'Woodstock', 'Our House', 'Country Girl' and 'Everybody I Love You'

Dallas Taylor: drums on all tracks except 'Teach Your Children' and '4+20', tambourine on 'Teach Your Children'

Jerry Garcia: pedal steel guitar on 'Teach Your Children'

John Sebastian: harmonica on 'Déjà Vu'

Unknown: piano on 'Everybody I Love You'

Producers: Crosby, Stills, Nash & Young

Bill Halverson: engineer

Recorded at Wally Heider Studio 3, Hollywood & Wally Heider Studio San Francisco

Gary Burden: art direction and design

Henry Diltz, Tom Gundelfinger: photography

Label: Atlantic

Chart positions: UK: 5, US: 1

Following the huge impact of the first Crosby Stills & Nash album, expectations were high. The pre-release sales topped $2 million. That put pressure on everybody. The circumstances of the entire band had changed on a personal level. On the first album, all three group members were in steady, stable relationships. That had been blown apart. Joni Mitchell, who had been discovered by David Crosby and had an affair with him, had spent two years with Graham Nash. They'd been talking about marriage when, in a change of heart, she began to feel stifled and left the relationship. Her album *Blue* was a result of that breakup. Graham was left bereft. He was a vital element in the band. Not only did he contribute some of their most memorable songs and those stunning harmonies, but he was the glue that held the band together. He was always in the control room, giving out encouragement and suggestions. As Neil says in *Waging Heavy Peace*: 'Graham was the consummate professional'.

Stephen Stills had been having a tumultuous love affair with the singer Judy Collins. He'd written the gorgeous love song 'Suite: Judy Blue Eyes' for her. She was based in New York, while Stephen was based in Los Angeles; she had just reclaimed custody of her child from her first marriage and decided that that was more important than their relationship, so she left. Yet, Stephen's musical prowess and the intense way that he and Neil fed off each other were crucial to the way the band performed. He and Neil might have had their problems, but together, they were dynamite. Neil, very diplomatically, says in his autobiography: 'Stephen, my brother, always the soulful conflicted one, battling demons, contributing an edge that was unmistakable'.

David Crosby's situation was even direr. He had broken up his relationship with Christine Hinton to have an affair with Joni Mitchell, but they got back together and were very serious. Christine had been driving David's VW van to take their cats to the vet. One escaped and, in a panic, jumped onto her. She lost control of the van and veered into a head-on collision with a school bus and was killed. David was heartbroken and often in tears. Yet, David was still the powerhouse of the band. Neil comments in *Waging Heavy Peace*: 'Crosby was forever the catalyst. Always intense, driving us further and further'.

Bringing Neil into the mix, with his and Stephen's past history of intense rivalry, probably did not help. Stephen was still in his manic phase, playing a multitude of instruments and filling every single space in the music, creating a folk version of Spector's Wall Of Sound. In an interview for *Rolling Stone*: 'Steve's whole thing right now is the group', Young says. 'It'd be impossible to have everybody into it as much as him. It'd be bedlam'.

Neil certainly brought some added quality to the album with both his songwriting and musicianship. He was a fully-fledged member of the band. Interestingly, drummer Dallas Taylor and bassist Greg Reeves played on nearly all the tracks but were never seen as being part of the band. Their names do appear on the album, but in smaller letters. That was probably because they were not seen as adding to the creativity that led to the songs. Their roles were purely to deliver their musical parts.

There was not a great deal of mixing together either socially or professionally. All the individual members would record their own songs and bring them in for the others to add instrumentation and vocals. Not ideal. There was a lot of overdubbing and elaborations that, consequently, led to a rather overdone, even portentous, album. Neil explained to Jimmy McDonough in *Shakey*: 'What started out to be the world's greatest rock 'n' roll band became trying to be the richest rock 'n' roll band'.

There was a lot of vying for getting songs onto the album. A huge number were tried out and rejected. There was a meticulous attitude to the material, with songs being rerecorded and worked on incessantly in order to get them as near to perfect as was humanly possible. Stephen Stills said that there were 800 hours of studio time in the making of the album. The 50th Anniversary four-CD release, with its three CDs of alternative takes, demos and outtakes, is testimony to that. Some brilliant songs were left off the album.

The critical response was that a lot of the album was too saccharine-sweet and that Neil's contribution added some grit. However, Crosby, Stills, Nash & Young were the epitome of their time, reflecting the appearance, attitudes and philosophy of the sixties counterculture. They connected. They came from the time of the sixties LA underground and espoused its ethos. This was a time of great social upheaval, with a generation espousing new liberal attitudes towards, sex, drugs and spirituality; an age of freedom, experimentation and great optimism. This was the age of civil rights, equality, environmental awareness and anti-war. The young generation felt themselves to be creating a new, better, peaceful and meaningful way of living. The band reflected this; the music resonated, reflecting their values, thoughts and feelings. Neil expresses this sentiment in his autobiography: 'That was Crosby, Stills, Nash & Young to me. The connection to our generation was profound and we could feel it. I loved all those guys. We were all friends experiencing a phenomenon together'.

Neil was not completely happy with the CSNY experience and their musical ethos. Neil told Jimmy McDonough in *Shakey*: 'Dallas couldn't play my shit for crap. Dallas was really Stephen's drummer. Their thing was playing a lot of notes. Compared to the CSN&Y extravaganza, Crazy Horse was gutter trash'.

He preferred playing Crazy Horse's raw rock 'n' roll and found the perfectionism of CSN&Y too suffocating.

'Carry On' (Stephen Stills)

According to Graham Nash, they were short of an opener for the album and certainly got one with this Stills number. He went away and came back with two songs he had previously offered to Buffalo Springfield. He took the two, one of which was a modified version of 'Questions', and melded them together with a jam session in the studio. Stills plays the bulk of the instruments on this track, working with Dallas Taylor on drums and overdubbing acoustic and electric guitars, bass and extra percussion. It's almost a one-man band. The harmonies were then overdubbed and Neil only has a minor overdubbed guitar.

What immediately comes across is the meticulous precision that is being applied. The acoustic guitars, with that fast underlying rhythm section in the background, provide a multi-textured platform over which the amazingly tight and utterly wonderful harmonies shine. Stephen embellishes this with the most fluid electric guitar.

The bridge between the two songs takes the form of a jam, including the acapella phrasing 'Carry on, Love is coming, Love is coming to us all' vocal section, which successfully evolves from the faster pace of 'Carry On' to the slower pace of the modified 'Questions'. There is a small section of Neil's edgy guitar overdub, but then we're back with Stills doing his wah-wah guitar over the 'Questions' section.

The result is an upbeat number that works well as a lively opener that is full of energy. It ended up as the B-side of the first single 'Teach Your Children'.

'Teach Your Children' (Graham Nash)

The song was written by Graham Nash in 1968 after having seen a photograph by Diane Arbus, of a child playing with a toy hand grenade. It made him question what we were teaching our children about war and violence.

The song is given a bouncy country vibe by Stephen Stills, emphasised by Jerry Garcia's country-style steel guitar contributions. In *Waging Heavy Peace*, Neil explains how Jerry came to be involved: 'Jerry Garcia came in and played a steel guitar part. It was actually a regular guitar with a slide. He just sat under the speakers with it on his lap and put that part on'. Jerry agreed to come in and perform the steel guitar part, which he did in one take, in exchange for them schooling the Grateful Dead in harmonies for their next album.

The soft acoustic bed of guitars, playing to a tambourine beat, underlies the whole piece. The social message, the sixties code on the road of peace and love, is cocooned within the most silky of vocals, with immaculate harmonies. If only all the world leaders had been brought up with this message.

As for Neil's part in it, as he says in *Waging Heavy Peace*, he was in the control room watching the whole event unfold. 'Crosby, Stills & Nash sang perfectly without me! I was in the control room'.

'Almost Cut My Hair' (David Crosby)

The band adopted a much heavier electric sound on this track: a slow, edgy anthem. This is David taking a clear stance on aligning himself with the anti-establishment counterculture and 'Letting my freak flag fly'. The lyrics and music reflect the tensions that existed in society at the time, with the student protests against the Vietnam War, the civil rights movement, the violence and paranoia. The 'us and them' divisions in society have rarely been greater. David was clearly taking sides.

The whole band were together when recording this, with Neil playing a prominent role by adding guitar parts. The vocals were all David's. Right up to the end, he never cut that hair and maintained his rebellious attitude. He kept his freak flag flying just like he said he would.

'Helpless' (Neil Young)

I guess we're all helpless before the forces of time and nature; it just takes someone like Neil to say it. The track is extremely laid back, with some eerie steel guitar and Neil's vulnerable, expressive voice resonating over that slow dirge to create a primal feel that was utterly hypnotic. Neil revealed his frustration in his autobiography:

Although it is a very simple song, it requires laying back, which was not really in Dallas Taylor's musical vocabulary that night. I just kept doing it over and over, waiting for him to settle down on drums and stop playing accents and fills everywhere.

Neil is rarely happy, but he was more than satisfied with Stephen's contribution as he explained in *Waging Heavy Peace*. 'Stephen played beautiful piano on the track while I sang it live'. Yet, he was slightly critical of Greg: 'Greg on bass was always in the pocket, although he played a lot of notes'. He seemed to be working well with Stephen. There was obviously mutual respect. 'In the next session, Stephen added a guitar with a volume pedal and it was a really fine part'. It was reported that the band had to record this track a number of times because they were so coked up that they had to wait for it to wear off before they could get it right.

'Woodstock' (Joni Mitchell)
Joni wrote this for the wonder that was Woodstock, but Crosby, Stills, Nash & Young, who played at the event (Neil slunk in the background and refused to be filmed), made it their own. Joni was due to perform at the festival but pulled out at the last minute because her manager thought she would not get back in time to appear on a prestigious *Dick Calvert Show*. She wrote the song in frustration after watching the Woodstock concert live on TV and having an excited report from her partner, Graham Nash, after Crosby, Stills, Nash & Young had played their set.

CSN&Y give the track a hard rock treatment, starting with Neil's scary guitar and the hard beat of the rhythm section, settling into Stephen's smooth vocals and those scintillating background harmonies. There's an urgency and hard edge to this performance, with its allusions to the Cold War nuclear threat, as opposed to the peace and love of the concertgoers. At the time, nobody realised that this would be the apotheosis of the hippie dream, and from here on, it was all downhill.

'Déjà Vu' (David Crosby)
David said to *The Guardian* in 2008: 'I'm one of those people who think we go round again. The Buddhists have got it right – it's a wheel and we get on and get off. I think life energy gets recycled. That's why I wrote 'Déjà Vu'. Let's hope he's right and that incredible voice has not been silenced forever.

The track starts with that circular pattern of acoustic guitars before almost resetting itself. What follows is a psychedelic melange of acoustic guitars, grooving, bubbling bass and ghostly, interjecting vocal parts. The track changes, develops and evolves at a moment's notice, floating along in a simultaneously controlled and chaotic manner. Then, the piece is given an ominous touch with lines such as 'Feel Like I've been here before' and 'What's going on?' – a neverending cycle. It seems that David's different takes were so

111

different in time signatures and laden with inconsistencies that the piece had to be assembled like a jig-saw from multiple flawed takes.

'Our House' (Graham Nash)

Graham Nash wrote this about an idyllic scene from his time living with Joni Mitchell, a record of an everyday event. They had stopped at an antique shop where they had bought a vase that Joni had liked. Reaching home, Graham had said to Joni that if she picked some flowers for the vase, he'd light the fire. Hours later, this simple act was immortalised in a sweet song. Very twee but compelling, it paints a picture of the domestic bliss of two love-struck lovers in the early stages of a relationship. A picture that was sadly spoilt a short time later when Joni left, leaving Graham distraught.

It starts slowly, with Graham singing the first verse in a gentle tone over scattered piano notes. The piano then sets up a simple repeating motif that is maintained throughout as the vocal picks up. The band come in instrumentally with a warm, slow, booming bass and slow, steady drumbeat. Stephen and David add backing vocals – slow and easy with a series of 'la's. The end lines are delivered solo, with just those sparse piano notes, ending with a chord. It's all very sweet, perfectly delivered, quite adorable, if a tad slushy. You're left with a warm glow, but it could give you diabetes in large doses.

'4 + 20' (Stephen Stills)

This delicate, haunting song is a solo effort from Stephen. He recorded it in one take, although he wanted to re-record it because he wasn't happy with a minor verbal stumble towards the end. He had to be persuaded that it was fine as it was. The song is perfectly crafted and sung in Stephen's most mellow voice, laden with emotion – a melodic masterpiece. The delicately picked guitar rings with perfectly formed notes.

The lyrics are simple. They tell the story of a man who watched his father work hard to support his family but always lived in strife. Now, Stephen, as a man of 24, finds himself beset by a different kind of poverty, one of the heart and soul. He's driven to desperation by the loss of a woman and his life is now empty and meaningless. It's pretty heavy subject matter for such a tender song. One might assume it was another eulogy for the departed Judy. However, Stephen put a slightly different gloss on it by suggesting it was written for an 84-year-old man 'who started and finished with nothing'.

'Country Girl: Whiskey Boot Hill/Down, Down, Down/Country Girl (I Think You're Pretty)' (Neil Young)

Neil recorded this track with Greg Reeves and Dallas Taylor, deliberately excluding the others. It was recorded live in the studio in his usual 'believe in the music' manner. The backing vocals were then overdubbed later.

The song, related to 'Broken Arrow', has three distinct sections that were spawned in Neil's earlier songs. The fact that it is described in the title as three songs was supposed to have earned Neil more writing credits on the album. I don't know if that was the intent.

The first section 'Whiskey Boot Hill' was released as an instrumental string quartet arrangement on Neil's first album. It was performed with lyrics acoustically on *Live At The Riverboat* in 1969. The second section, 'Down Down Down', which forms the bulk of the song, was recorded with Buffalo Springfield but remained unreleased until the box set was released in 2001. The final verse is 'Country Girl (I Think You're Pretty)'.

This is one of Neil's five-minute epics. The piano leads into Neil's plaintive vocal. The drums are restrained, creating a relaxed rhythm. The strings come in to transform this into a lush production. At first, Neil's vocal is very controlled, delicate and beautiful, even though the track retains a raw edge. The wonderful harmonies start in a reserved manner, but build as the track progresses. It changes as it goes into the 'Down Down Down' section, with some immaculate vocal overdubs. By the end, it has built into an instrumental wall of sound. When the short 'Country Girl' section comes in, the organ is more prominent. Then, the wailing harmonica sends shivers through you. The varying intensity and instrumentation create more sophistication for the lilting melodies; at times haunting, other times powerful. However, this extravaganza failed to impress Neil, who described the end result, with all of its overdubs, as overblown.

As to the content: well, Boot Hill is where the cowboys were buried with their boots on and the whiskey bars are where the stars hang out waiting to die. The waitresses move between the tables and flirt with the customers for tips. The song is concerned with this unbalanced relationship. Neil seems to have a thing about waitresses. He spent a lot of time with friends, picking up girls in bars. His first wife, Susan Acevedo, was the owner/hostess in the canyon who used to serve him breakfast every day. In *Waging Heavy Peace*, Neil describes how he met up with Susan.

> I used to go to the Canyon Kitchen every morning for breakfast. Susan Acevedo, the beautiful Sicilian hostess/owner, would bring me a one-eye and bacon. I got to look at Susan Acevedo every day at breakfast!

His wife Pegi, whom he met in 1974 and married in 1978, was also a waitress.

The second section moves into a darker mode of unfaithfulness, remorse, guilt and difficulty in providing forgiveness due to lack of trust (even though he is guilty of the same infidelity).

The third section is the simple yearning for a pretty girl to come and share his simple life in the cabin in the canyon.

'Everybody I Love You' (Stephen Stills, Neil Young)
A crisp three-minute end to the album. Appropriately, a collaboration between Stills and Young. Set to a driving beat, with a monster of a bass from Greg,

this has everything, from Neil's raw, stinging guitar, Stephen's soaring vocal and the superb, characteristic, signature CSNY harmonies.

Stephen's telling his girl to stop being defensive, to stop hiding away, to open up and let him in. He means her no harm. He loves her. He's shouting it to the world, opening it out, in the whole widest context of the prevailing sixties hippie dream, to include everyone – 'Everybody I love you!'. What better ending could you have?

Singles
'Woodstock' (Joni Mitchell) b/w **'Helpless'** (Neil Young)
The first single released was lifted straight off the album and intended to maximise the Woodstock vibe with a cover of the Joni Mitchell song, eulogising and immortalising the gathering. The B-side was Neil's wavering masterpiece of a song 'Helpless'. The single captured the prevailing mood and went straight to number one.

'Teach Your Children' (Graham Nash) b/w **'Carry On'** (Stephen Stills)
The second single was the Graham Nash song 'Teach Your Children', which also tapped into the prevalent Hippie wave. That same vibe was carried on with Stephen's B-side. 'Teach Your Children' went straight into the charts and might have reached number one if it had not been undermined by the release of the next CSN&Y single, rushed out while 'Teach Your Children' was still climbing.

'Ohio' (Neil Young) b/w **'Find The Cost Of Freedom'** (Stephen Stills)
This was the first non-album single. 'Ohio' had been written by Neil in response to the Ohio Kent State massacre, where State Troopers shot four peacefully protesting students dead. This was Neil's response to seeing the picture of Mary Ann Vecchio kneeling distraught over the body of the young student Jeffrey Miller, who had been gunned down by State Troopers. Gerald Casale from Devo had been there on that day. Jimmy McDonough, in *Shakey,* relates an interview with someone present at the Kent State massacre:

> Two of the four people who were killed, Jeffrey Miller and Allison
> Krause, were my friends. We were all running our arses off from those
> motherfuckers. It was total, utter bullshit. Live ammunition and gasmasks –
> none of us knew, none of us could have imagined… They shot into a crowd
> that was running away from them.

Neil wrote this song in a fit of fury, shared it with the others, recorded it the next day and rushed it out as a single, despite the fact that 'Teach Your Children' was still going up the charts. They thought 'Ohio' was too important and relevant to wait. Neil eulogised to Jimmy McDonough about the recording of the track: "Ohio' is the best record I ever made with Crosby,

Stills, Nash & Young. Definitely. That's the only recording I know where
CSN&Y is really a band'.

The B-side is the sad counterpoint to the fury of Neil's invective. Stephen
wrote this epitaph as a fitting tribute – a single, poignant verse. It starts with
Stephen's beautifully picked acoustic guitar. Other acoustic guitars come in
to set up a stunning interaction full of delicate melodies. In unison, a gang
of vocals enter, sung over a soft acoustic in the background. They repeat
the verse. This time, the guitar drops out and, with real power and intensity,
they sing the verse a cappella and now with harmonies. The venom pours in
saccharine streams of golden voices. 'Find the cost of freedom buried in the
ground. Mother Earth will swallow you. Lay your body down'.

'Our House' (Graham Nash) b/w **'Déjà Vu'** (David Crosby)
The last single from this period was, again, lifted directly off the album,
sharing out the writing credits. By now, most people had a copy of this huge-
selling album, but it still climbed into the Top 20.

Conclusion
Amazingly, given all the trials and tribulations, personality clashes and
difficulties, the album was completed and came out sounding great. A four-
CD 50th anniversary box set was released in 2021, containing numerous
outtakes, alternative versions and demos, most of which did not feature Neil
at all. Only two of these tracks are of note in the context of Neil. The first is
a demo of 'Birds' featuring a duo with Graham Nash and the second is an
alternative version of 'Helpless' featuring a harmonica.

Four-Way Street (1971)

Personnel:
David Crosby: vocals, guitar
Stephen Stills: vocals, guitar, piano, organ
Graham Nash: vocals, guitar, piano, organ
Neil Young: vocals, guitar
Calvin 'Fuzzy' Samuels: bass
Johnny Barbata: drums
Producers: David Crosby, Stephen Stills, Graham Nash, Neil Young
Bill Halverson: engineer
Gary Burden: art direction/design, photography
Joel Bernstein: photography centre squares
Henry Diltz: inside sleeve photography
Live recording at Fillmore East, NY, 2-7 June 1970, The Forum, LA, 26-28 June 1970, Chicago Auditorium, 5 July 1970
Label: Atlantic
Chart positions: UK: 5, US: 1

Although this wasn't released until 1971, it has been culled from concerts in June and July 1970, so I reckon it fits within this brief and makes a fitting end to Neil's sixties period. *Four Way Street* was released as a double album featuring live tracks from recordings made in New York at the Fillmore East, in L.A. at The Forum and in Chicago at the Auditorium Theatre. Just imagine how much material, beautifully recorded, is still sitting in vaults. All those concerts were recorded in full.

The album features many songs that were, as yet, unreleased, but which would shortly come out on their various solo ventures. Neil had a couple that would shortly see the light of day on *Everybody Knows This Is Nowhere*. It also featured their single 'Ohio' with B-side 'Find The Cost Of Freedom'. At the time, Neil was juggling, by agreement, three distinct and separate career threads. There was his acoustic solo career, his band Crazy Horse and now CSN&Y. The others were juggling, too. It's no wonder that emotions were running high. There was a lot of overlap of material with CSN&Y and individual solo efforts. What is interesting is to hear the differences between the different versions.

Looking back, it is incredible that the band managed to perform and that an album of such quality was created, given the turmoil and internal friction within the band. That mayhem began right from the beginning of the tour. Firstly, Greg Reeves was fired, ostensibly because instead of keeping the right rhythm, he was going off on his own complicated runs, but probably because he was getting too full of himself and wanting to perform his own songs with the band. He was replaced with Calvin 'Fuzzy' Samuels (a homeless Jamaican musician discovered by Stills in the studios at Island Records in London). Then, Dallas Taylor was sacked by Neil, ostensibly because he could not keep a consistent tempo, but more likely because of his flirting with Susan Acevedo, Neil's wife. John Barbata, from The Turtles, replaced him.

The constant bickering and arguments between the band members, fueled by Stills' heavy cocaine and alcohol use, came to a head when Stills went off on an extended solo set in order to impress Bob Dylan, who was in the audience. The other three fired Stills. He was soon reinstated, though, in order to complete the tour. At the end of the gruelling tour, not surprisingly, amid claims of megalomania and ego-driven madness, the band split up. What we are left with is a legacy of genius created in a cauldron of molten egos.

The album demonstrates the raw power that Neil added to what was a sublime amalgamation of voices and electric and acoustic instruments. Sides one and two are acoustic, whilst sides three and four are electric. All four sides are equally brilliant. This track listing is taken from the CD release with the additional four bonus tracks ('King Midas In Reverse', 'Laughing', 'Black Queen' and 'The Loner/Cinnamon Girl/Down By The River' medley)

'Suite: Judy Blue Eyes' (Stephen Stills)
Thirty-four seconds of the end 'doo doo's of the harmony of 'Suite: Judy Blue Eyes' fading in, building to full volume! The end was the beginning.

'On The Way Home' (Neil Young)
Three acoustic guitars and three voices, with Graham standing to the side. The trio joust as Neil takes the lead vocal and Steve plays the guitar solo.

'Teach Your Children' (Graham Nash)
Graham takes the lead vocal on this, with some great acoustic guitar interaction and harmonising backing vocals. There's a charming giggle at the 'you of tender years' line and, at one point, they even get the audience to clap along.

'Triad' (David Crosby)
David's been looking for a home for this song for a while. It was recorded with The Byrds but was then kept from being included on *The Notorious Byrd Brothers* following his firing from the band. Jefferson Airplane recorded it on *Crown Of Creation*. CSN&Y recorded it in the studio, but it wasn't included on the *Déjà Vu* album (that version finally came out in the 50th anniversary *Déjà Vu* box set). Finally, it gets a release here.

The theme is a very sixties one of a ménage a trois and includes some references to Robert Heinlein's *Stranger In A Strange Land* – a tale of free love: 'sister, lovers, some you must know about water brothers – grok?' and 'But I don't really see – why can't we go on as three?'

Following a little burst of beautifully picked guitar and a spoken intro, David delivers this delicate song solo, with a voice as clear as a bell and a slow-strummed guitar.

'The Lee Shore' (David Crosby)

This track pictures David on the shore at sunset, relishing the beauty, looking at the sparkling shells, wheelin' gulls and dreaming about the islands – 'A hundred thousand islands flung like jewels upon the sea' – where he could escape with his woman and live free. He had a sailboat and loved sailing between the islands. He is rudely awoken from his reveries by the women calling him for a meal. David delivers this gentle gem to a simple guitar refrain, the others joining to blend their voices and soar like angels – wonderful.

The song was recorded by CSNY in 1969 at Stephen Stills' home studio, but it wasn't released. Later, they added vocal overdubs to it and the track came out on two compilations – *Carry On* and *CSN*.

'Chicago' (Graham Nash)

This is Graham Nash's political song, dedicated to Mayor Daley, about the Chicago riots at the Democratic Convention in 1968. Many youth groups, including the anti-war protestors, the Yippies and Black Panthers, went to Chicago to protest the Vietnam War, civil rights and the political system in a mass, non-violent gathering. They were met with tear gas and heavy-handed batons from riot police. The eight organisers were charged with conspiracy to riot, which led to the trial of 'The Chicago Eight' (which included Jerry Rubin, Abbie Hoffman, Phil Ochs and Bobby Seale). Bobby Seale, the Blank Panther leader, kept interrupting proceedings with protesting outbursts, so the judge ordered him to be gagged and tied to his chair.

Outraged at the violent way that Mayor Daley had dealt with the protest, Graham Nash wrote this song. It begins with a simple repeating piano motif over which Graham's forceful vocal is sung. The rest of the group vocally join in to reinforce the end of lines and the chorus: 'We can change the world! Rearrange the world! It's dying! It's dying! To get better!' The piano accompaniment becomes more strident, pounding and assertive as the voices blend and soar into exquisite harmonies, remaining strong and firm.

This was the sixties. There were clear sides. The young were against the old, opposing the war and the capitalist society. These were the days of idealism and optimism when people really thought that they could take on the establishment and change the world. Graham's song reflected all that – the taking of sides, the identification with the anti-war movement, the civil rights movement and the protests. Music was the centre of the youth culture. It meant a lot. They got the crowd clapping along in sympathy and generated a big roar of approval at the end. 'Rules and regulation, who needs them? Throw 'em all out the door'. We were making a new set of rules.

The song featured on Graham's shortly-to-be-released debut album and was put out as a single.

'Right Between The Eyes' (Graham Nash)

This is a song about honesty in communication and relationships. Graham said that he wrote the song in response to a relationship he'd had with a woman who he later found out was married. It might also refer to the stormy relationships going on within the band. A soft, tender song of hurt, the track features slow, warm, strummed and picked guitar, with Graham's quiet, intense vocal augmented by some gorgeous interweaving harmonies.

'Cowgirl In The Sand' (Neil Young)

This is a solo acoustic version of the classic Neil Young song from his recent *Everybody Knows This Is Nowhere* album. That familiar refrain starts up, with the guitar having some beautiful bass bottom end and then Neil's firm, wavery vocal comes in – a great version.

'Don't Let It Bring You Down' (Neil Young)

We are served up another dose of Neil – a solo acoustic version of a new song. This is from his, as of that time, unreleased album *After The Gold Rush*. He introduces it with the words: 'This is a new song, guaranteed to bring you right down, called 'Don't Let It Bring You Down'. It starts out real slow and then fizzles out altogether', which elicits a laugh from the crowd.
It certainly doesn't fizzle out, building in intensity to produce a fine version. The competition, rivalry and mutual respect within the group seem to bring out the best in all of them. This is no exception.

'49 Bye-Byes'/'America's Children' (Stephen Stills)

Neil introduces Stephen as a good friend and acknowledges that they've had their differences. Stephen then goes to the piano and starts off with a slow, moody version of '49 Bye-Byes' – one of Stephen's sad songs about parting ways with Judy Collins. The mood changes. The piano speeds up to a frantic pace and he incites the crowd to clap along and get involved, launching into the frenetic first verse of 'For What It's Worth'. This then transitions into a highly charged political diatribe/rap about Richard Nixon, Spiro Agnew and Mayor Daley, nailing his flag to the youth revolution and protests, telling them that 'America's still the home of the brave'. He reminds them that young people are being shot down protesting in the streets but motivates them to 'Keep on keeping on!', proclaiming that 'Jesus Christ was the first non-violent revolutionary'. Finally, we arrive back to the final verses of 'For What It's Worth' at breakneck speed, ending with rapturous applause. It seems that every band member feels the need to firmly align themselves with the youth revolution.

'Love The One You're With' (Stephen Stills)

The whole band come together to supply acoustic guitar and backing vocals for this Stephen Stills number. It's a speedy version, with the meshing guitars producing a wall of sound to underscore Stephen's intense voice. It sounds like they're all on speed or even coke. This is a track that features on Stephen's soon-to-be-released debut album *Stephen Stills*.

'King Midas In Reverse' (Graham Nash, Allan Clarke, Tony Hicks)

Although credited to Graham and other members of The Hollies, this was actually just a Graham Nash composition. Graham, armed with an acoustic guitar, carries out a solo performance of this Hollies hit, a song about a relationship coming to an end, leaving him in despair. Everything he touches turns to dust.

It is probably my least favourite track on the album – it sounds lightweight to me.

'Laughing' (David Crosby)

This was a song that David wrote for his good friend George Harrison after George had told him about the Maharishi. David, who didn't believe in god or religion, was very sceptical.

> Take it with a grain of salt. Don't just accept it at face value. So, I wrote that song to tell him that. That the person I thought was the wisest I had met was a child laughing at the sun. And I thought I could learn more from that child laughing at the sun than I could from anybody teaching.

For some reason, George did not record the song. I wonder why? This is a solo effort by David that starts with a dirge-like guitar, with Croz's dreamy, lilting voice. The track would later come out on his debut album *If I Could Only Remember My Name* ....

'Black Queen' (Stephen Stills)

Stephen comes out with his acoustic. 'Gonna do a Country Blues. Music from back home'. He proceeds to tell a short story about a Black blues man back in Louisiana, before launching into a very raw and powerful blues. He showcases some excellent sharp guitar work and mumbles, hums and sings over the guitar in true blues fashion, stifling some laughs from the audience with the aside, 'one thing blues ain't is funny'.

'The Loner, Cinnamon Girl, Down By The River' (Neil Young)

Neil completes the side with a nine-minute plus medley of 'The Loner' from *Neil Young* and 'Cinnamon Girl' and 'Down By The River' from *Everybody Knows This Is Nowhere*. 'The Loner' starts with some great guitar, with a lot of bottom end and slashing chords creating a warm sound, and Neil's voice is anguished and his delivery forceful. It builds as it progresses, then slides effortlessly without pause or link. With a few chord changes, we are into a more uplifting mood with 'Cinnamon Girl'. The voice alternates between sounding fragile in that higher register and strong in the chorus, as he ploughs out those power chords on his acoustic. The tempo then slows. A few bridging chords take us into the slower 'Down By The River'. Neil builds the intensity with some heavy strums as he approaches the chorus, which he delivers with heartbreaking passion. This medley concludes the acoustic section and Neil steals the show.

'Pre-Road Downs' (Graham Nash)
The electric section opens with some muted chords on electric guitar setting the beat, before the full band launch into a heavy version of Graham's song about leaving home and loved ones to go out on the road. 'Pre-Road Downs' was from the Crosby, Stills & Nash debut album from 1969. In this performance, the band produce a seriously heavy version, with driving drums and soaring guitars.

'Long Time Gone' (David Crosby)
The drums and some edgy, loud guitar kick things off, with the prominent bass picking an elaborate path before emphasising the beat, all underpinned by the organ. The number has numerous changes of pace and intensity, as it proceeds with quiet passages and frenzied playing, demonstrating that the band can really rock! David takes the vocal on this highly political number, in which he exhorts the crowd to 'speak out against the madness'. David explains the song (released on their first album *Crosby, Stills & Nash*) in the liner notes:

> It was written the night Bobby Kennedy was killed. I believed in him because he said he wanted to make some positive changes in America, and he hadn't been bought and sold like Johnson and Nixon – cats who made their deals years ago with the special interests in this country in order to gain power. I thought Bobby, like his brother, was a leader who had not made those deals. I was already angry about Jack Kennedy getting killed and it boiled over into this song when they got his brother, too.

'Southern Man' (Neil Young)
A powerful, full-blooded version of this rousing, politically charged song. Neil is in fine voice and it gives him space to extemporise his guitar work. The rest of the band is in full support, both musically and with backing vocals. There is some exceptional playing in the nearly 14-minute instrumental section, as the band jam and bring out the best in each other. Stills and Young work so well together. They seem to dare each other to do more. The rhythm section holds it all together as they jam in a scintillating show of instrumental proficiency. Crosby, Stills, Nash & Young had a reputation as a political band, and this song about slavery and racism in the Southern States fits right into that category.

'Ohio' (Neil Young)

The strong political protest continues. You could only follow something as strong as 'Southern Man' with something even more charged. This burst of anger is suitably incandescent – they nail it

'Carry On' (Stephen Stills)

The heavy political theme is further continued in a different way with this Stephen Stills masterpiece. The band deliver a perfect rendition, complete with harmonies, wah-wah guitar, storming electricity and compelling singing from Stills, of this *Déjà Vu* classic. 'We have no choice but to carry on'. They transform it into a statement of intent. The song develops into another extended jam, with the melding of the instruments jiving with the thundering bass and a steady, forceful drumbeat. The platform of the solid rhythm section gives the three guitarists room to jam in the course of this 14-minute epic, in which they clearly demonstrate their individual prowess.

'Find The Cost Of Freedom' (Stephen Stills)

For the last track, they all gather together with their acoustic guitars to exchange some delicious licks on this tender track. Their four voices blend together in this beautiful, melodic, hymn-like requiem. It makes a suitable, poignant finale for what is an exceptional live album.

Conclusion

Four-Way Street, as the name suggests, has been a platform for the four outstanding talents that were Neil Young, Stephen Stills, David Crosby and Graham Nash. The first side may have, at times, appeared more like a conglomeration of adverts for forthcoming solo ventures, but nonetheless, it still shines. The worth of those individuals was such that it worked; it provided both quality and variety. At the times when those four people (six on the live sides) came together, either acoustically or electrically, the result was magical. There was sheer synergy. They acted as catalysts for each other and became greater than the sum of their parts.

The sad thing is that the band imploded. Instead of a follow-up to *Déjà Vu*, there were a flurry of solo albums, various combinations of members and a continuing history of drugs and feuds. Despite numerous attempts, it wasn't until 1988, with *American Dream*, that the four of them would come back together to make a studio album.

Neil set about carving out his highly successful solo career, starting with the massive *Harvest* – he became the most successful of them all.

Neil Young Archives Vol. 1 1963-1972

The archives started with the *Decades* retrospective. Neil had the desire to scour the vaults and gather together all the tracks to reflect the whole of his career. Strangely, for someone who could be incredibly picky about his output and, at times, exceptionally meticulous about every facet of his work and life, Neil was not too precious. He wanted this archive to reflect the whole of his colossal output: the good, the okay and the downright quirky. He said that he wanted people to hear the alternative takes and rejected songs so that they could hear for themselves why they were passed over.

The archives were an enormous project, much bigger than Neil could manage on his own; therefore, he appointed Joel Bernstein to oversee the venture. Joel had been an obsessive fan who had been brought into the inner fold, a man who knew Neil Young's career inside out. What he didn't know didn't exist. It made for quite a rocky set of arguments, but the end result was very fruitful. The archives are intended to collect everything together – the demos, alternative takes, unreleased songs and live material. Of course, it could not possibly contain everything. That would be ridiculous. But it does gather together enough to paint the picture of how Neil's career has developed and brought to light much material that was previously unavailable, except on scuzzy bootlegs.

So far, there are two volumes of the archives. Neil is aiming for five – each one roughly representing a decade in Neil's career. The one that is pertinent to this book is the first one *Neil Young Archives Vol. 1 1963-1972*. It takes us from Neil's first musical ventures with The Squires, through his early solo material, his stint with Buffalo Springfield, into his later solo work, his work with Crazy Horse, then Crosby, Stills, Nash & Young and beyond. While everything is not there – The Mynah Birds, for instance – it does provide a very satisfying, pretty comprehensive picture of the spectrum of Neil's work in the early years.

Neil wanted the project to represent his music in excellent sound quality, therefore, he ensured that the sources and product were as good as he could get. *Volume 1* was released as a multimedia set, either as ten Blu-ray discs, as ten DVDs or as eight CDs. As well as his music, it also contained his film efforts – such as the full-length *Journey Through The Past*.

Unfortunately, the set was only released as a limited edition and fetches high prices. The other annoying thing is that the live sets were released as stand-alone CDs, in Neil's Performance Series, prior to the archives coming out, so that now, for people that bought those live sets earlier, there is a lot of duplication.

However, this messing with the past resulted in other Neil Young projects. Neil decided to set up an online archive that is even more comprehensive and offers high-quality streaming of all his material. That site is exceptional. His sadly deceased manager Elliot Roberts stated that it cost a million dollars to set up. I can believe that. Neil worked with archivist Hannah Johnson and

Toshi Onuki, a Tokyo-based art director, to make it something very special. On top of all that, Neil also set about producing an official bootleg series, in which he replicated the art and content of popular bootlegs and put them out with a high-quality upgrade.

All of the material on the first archives album has already been dealt with in the relevant sections of this book. However, this is the tracklisting:

CD 1 Early Years: 1963-1968
The Squires – 'Aurora', The Squires – 'The Sultan', The Squires – 'Mustang', The Squires – 'I'll Love You Forever', The Squires – '(I'm A Man And) I Can't Cry', Neil Young & Comrie Smith – 'Hello Lonely Woman', Neil Young & Comrie Smith – 'Casting Me Away From You', Neil Young & Comrie Smith – 'There Goes My Babe', Neil Young – 'Sugar Mountain', Neil Young – 'Nowadays Clancy Can't Even Sing', Neil Young – 'Runaround Babe', Neil Young – 'The Ballad Of Peggy Grover', Neil Young – 'The Rent Is Always Due', Neil Young – 'Extra, Extra', Neil Young – 'Flying On The Ground Is Wrong', Buffalo Springfield – 'Burned', Buffalo Springfield – 'Out Of My Mind', Neil Young – 'Down, Down, Down', Buffalo Springfield – 'Kahuna Sunset', Buffalo Springfield – 'Mr Soul', Buffalo Springfield – 'Sell Out', Buffalo Springfield – 'Down To The Wire', Neil Young – 'Expecting To Fly', Neil Young – 'Slowly Burning', Neil Young – 'One More Sign', Buffalo Springfield – 'Broken Arrow'

CD 2 Topanga 1: 1968-1969
Neil Young – 'I Am A Child', Neil Young – 'Everybody Knows This Is Nowhere', Neil Young – 'The Loner', Neil Young – 'Birds', Neil Young – 'What Did You Do To My Life?', Neil Young – 'The Last Trip To Tulsa', Neil Young – 'Here We Are In The Years', Neil Young – 'I've Been Waiting For You', Neil Young – 'The Old Laughing Lady', Neil Young – 'I've Loved Her So Long', Neil Young – 'Sugar Mountain', Neil Young – 'Nowadays Clancy Can't Even Sing', Neil Young With Crazy Horse – 'Down By The River', Neil Young With Crazy Horse – 'Cowgirl In The Sand', Neil Young With Crazy Horse – 'Everybody Knows This Is Nowhere'

CD 3 Live At The Riverboat: Toronto 1969
See tracklisting in Live Albums section.

CD 4 Topanga 2: 1969-1970
Neil Young With Crazy Horse – 'Cinnamon Girl', Neil Young With Crazy Horse – 'Running Dry (Requiem For The Rockets)', Neil Young With Crazy Horse – 'Round And Round (It Won't Be Long)', Neil Young With Crazy Horse – 'Oh Lonesome Me', Neil Young With Crazy Horse – 'Birds', Neil Young With Crazy Horse – 'Everybody's Alone', Neil Young With Crazy Horse – 'I Believe In You', Crosby, Stills, Nash & Young – 'Sea Of Madness', Neil Young With Crazy Horse – 'Dance Dance Dance', Crosby, Stills, Nash & Young – 'Country Girl', Crosby, Stills, Nash & Young - 'Whiskey Boot Hill'/'Down, Down', 'Down'/'Country Girl (I

Think You're Pretty)', Crosby, Stills, Nash & Young – 'Helpless', Neil Young With Crazy Horse – 'It Might Have Been'.

CD 5 Live At The Fillmore East: New York 1970
See tracklisting in Live Albums section

CD 6 Topanga 3: 1970
Neil Young – 'Tell Me Why', Neil Young – 'After The Gold Rush', Neil Young – 'Only Love Can Break Your Heart', Neil Young – 'Wonderin'', Neil Young – 'Don't Let It Bring You Down', Neil Young – 'Cripple Creek Ferry', Neil Young – 'Southern Man', Neil Young – 'Till The Morning Comes', Neil Young With Crazy Horse – 'When You Dance, I Can Really Love', Crosby, Stills, Nash & Young – 'Ohio', Crosby, Stills, Nash & Young – 'Only Love Can Break Your Heart', Crosby, Stills, Nash & Young – 'Tell Me Why', David Crosby – 'Music Is Love', Neil Young – 'See The Sky About To Rain'

CD 7 Live At Massey Hall: Toronto 1971
Outside the scope of this book

CD 8 North Country: 1971-1972
Outside the scope of this book

The Official Bootlegs

So far, there have been six releases in this series, but there are a lot more planned. The released CDs are all of 1970s shows. The only one that fits into the context of this book is the Carnie Hall release, featuring Neil's performance at Carnegie Hall, New York, on 4 December 1970. This was just a couple of days after Neil's last gig at The Cellar Door in Washington, DC.

Neil Young Carnegie Hall (1970)

Personnel:
Neil Young: vocals, guitar, piano
Produced: Neil Young, Niko Bolas
Recorded by: Henry Lewy
Direction: Elliot Roberts
Release Date: 2021
Label: Shakey Pictures Records
Chart positions: UK: 32, US: 145

This upgraded bootleg is a 24-track double album put out on double vinyl. As the content and performances are so similar to the Cellar Door performances, I do not intend to give a review of each track. They are all solo renditions with either guitar or piano. The performance and production are both excellent, on par with The Cellar Door performances. There are a few new songs, reflecting the broken state of his marriage, that would appear on *Harvest* – 'Old Man' (written about Louie Arillo – the Portuguese Ranch foreman at Broken Arrow), 'See The Sky About To Fall' and 'Bad Fog Of Loneliness'. The only other aspect worthy of mention is Neil storming off before the end of the first set, following a noisy interruption from some fans who had invaded the packed house through the fire doors. Here is the setlist:

Side One: 'Down By The River', 'Cinnamon Girl', 'I Am A Child', 'Expecting To Fly', 'The Loner', 'Wonderin''
Side Two: 'Helpless', 'Southern Man', 'Nowadays Clancy Can't Even Sing', 'Sugar Mountain'
Side Three: 'On The Way Home', 'Tell Me Why', 'Only Love Can Break Your Heart', 'Old Man', 'After The Gold Rush', 'Flying On The Ground Is Wrong'
Side Four: 'Cowgirl In The Sand', 'Don't Let It Bring You Down', 'Birds', 'Bad Fog Of Loneliness', 'Ohio', 'See The Sky About To Rain', 'Dance Dance Dance'

The Afterword

Neil has fought through his entire career for real music full of emotion, expression and soul. He rails against music that he feels is over-commercialised. He also wants us all to hear it with all the power and intensity that he hears in the studio. He's had a war on MP3s, CDs and random selections. For Neil, the music was created to sound fulsome and move the listener. An album was put together with great thought so that the tracks flow and complement each other. I get all that.

Certainly, sitting down with headphones, a great hi-fi system and a pristine analogue album, one experiences all the separation, warmth, power, intensity, complexity and nuance that an artist like Neil puts into his music. It transports you. It hits you in the heart and gut. However, I also know that I've been delighted to hear one of Neil's songs oscillating out of a far-off radio station and have been deliriously happy singing along at the top of my cracked old voice to a crappy CD or MP3 being played at a volume way past the capacity of the cheap old car player. Good music plays in the head and gut. It evokes nostalgia, memories, times and dreams. It makes you move! In my view, there's room for both.

As I come to the end of this book, I am filled with wonder. I have had the privilege of listening intently to every single track Neil produced in the sixties, to reacquaint myself, relive episodes of my life where this music formed the backdrop and discover new depths to the songs. Listening to music for enjoyment is one thing; listening to it to write something about it is something else. It's like I've had new ears.

The sixties was a seminal period for me. Those were days of political and social upheaval, of war, antiwar and civil rights, the start of the environmental movement and equality for women. There was a sexual revolution, a wave of liberalisation and a real questioning of the establishment and where it was heading. The immense upheaval was nothing short of a social revolution. Neil was not only living it but was one of its leading architects. His music and lyrics reflected the times.

For Neil, it was the formative decade. He entered it as a young kid hooked on the music of the day, turned on by rock 'n' roll and R&B. It invaded his mind. He formed his high school bands, like The Jades, formed a semi-professional covers band, The Squires, recorded his first compositions, became a solo folk singer, joined an R&B band, The Mynah Birds, then hit the heights, first with Buffalo Springfield, then Crosby, Stills, Nash & Young and Crazy Horse, before, finally, leaving the decade as a major solo artist and a member of one of the biggest rock acts on the planet. Few people are as adept in both the acoustic and electric arenas. Neil is a master in both. It had been a decade of hard graft learning the trade, highs and lows, failure and then huge success.

His success brought huge rewards and enabled him to indulge: a cabin/ranch in the country, filmmaking, a studio, a fleet of restored cars, a vintage train set, and, most important of all, the scope to produce the music he wanted, how he wanted it. But that success, with all its demands, coupled with his one-tracked approach to creating the music to the standard he demanded, took its toll. Relationships with band members, friends, colleagues, wives and lovers were often strained to breaking point. Neil isn't easy. Everything he does, from the meticulous restoration of a wreck of a vintage car, the planning and execution of a tour, to the production of a song, has to be carried out to his exact wishes. He's a hard taskmaster – as a number of people have attested. But without that driven personality, and desire to get things right, we would not have this immense body of work.

Unfortunately, the last 18 months of the sixties had been too much for his marriage. Susan Acevedo found herself a rock 'n' roll widow. Neil was either on the road, recording or rehearsing. The music came first. Three solo albums, two tours with Crazy Horse, *Déjà Vu* recordings with Crosby, Stills, Nash & Young and three tours with CSN&Y later, she'd had enough. Even when she was with him, she had to put up with multitudes of girls throwing themselves at Neil. It was all too much. When Neil moved out from Topanga to his Broken Arrow Ranch, he left a distraught and extremely jealous Susan behind. It was over. Neil's lifestyle, the women, the drinking and the drugs, were almost as notorious as his music. He lived the rock 'n' roll life to the full. He left the 1960s with a broken heart and a broken marriage, but with a soaring career ahead of him.

He soon started a new relationship with the actress Carrie Snodgrass, who had starred in the 1970 film *Diary Of A Mad Housewife*. He sent her a message to set up a date. Then she found him in hospital, laid up with a bad back and in a back brace. It brought out the nurse in her. 'I fell in love with Neil's pain'. The romance briefly blossomed and she moved into Broken Arrow – but that's another story. That needs harvesting later. The sixties were over. Neil strode forward into his highway of twists, turns and cul-de-sacs. Neil Young is one of rock's leviathans, right up there with Bob Dylan, The Beatles and The Stones. 'Be great or be gone', Richard Berry used to say. Neil chose to be great.

Bibliography

Neil Young, *Waging Heavy Peace* (Penguin, 2012)
Jimmy McDonough, *Shakey: Neil Young's Biography* (Vintage, 2003)
Editors of Rolling Stone, *Neil Young – The Rolling Stone Files* (Hyperion, 1994)
Scott Young, *Neil And Me* (Rogan House, 1984)